EGREGOROI

VALENTIN SCAVR

TRANSLATION BY I.S.M.

ISBN-13: 978-0-9997680-4-4

EGREGOROI

EGREGOROI

HERMON

I

1. The Light teach to know its legends;
The Light desires to preserve its being unchanged;
but we have seen in the twilight hour -
When the moon rises in the east -
as the Devil walks the earth,
And the Angels, Guardians of the Heavens,
Descendeth from skies, shaking the earthly realms,
Becoming the Devils...

2. Many winters ago, were among the men, who lived on the earth,
Those, who were elected by the Light, and its prophets,
Already decayed in the centuries, upon the northern winds,
They have written on pages of their epochs the covenants of biblical
Light,
Word by word they have gained the heavenly fire
From the glow of stars, burning in the sky -
And an only word of the Light was called by the name of truth.
And only submission to the Light was called by them a blessing;
And the Light itself.

3. But we have seen rebellion and proud, ascending from the
dismayed plains of the earth
But we have seen as stars descended from the skies one by one
As the sparks of heavenly fire
And they died into dusk, to never return again
on their places
But we have gazed as higher authorities were sworn to Satan
and from then become gods and devils for mankind
and concluded alliances between themselves
and took an oath of allegiance to each other in an eternal struggle
against the heavens...

4. And we saw how the Fallen walked among the sons of men,
enfleshed fire and confusion,
bringing them power, purity and pain of illumination,
tempting his humble soul;
We saw the young mankind,
Crossing the thresholds of laws,
Searching for the dark side, trying to get rid of grievous fetters
and the grim fate,
we have seen those whose immortal nature has fallen away from the
Light,
descending forever into the darkness
but hearts of only a few of those who have fallen, been able to ignite
to burn in constant opposition to the sky, sear it with bitterness and
anger...
Here we saw the Fallen,
rule among the first people as the gods of the ancient earth,
Granting to mankind dare and rapture, fulfillment of corruption of
being,
firmness of the outcast spirit
test of will...

5. We called the Fallen and honored with crimson sunset
Their majestic arrival,
we waited for the hour when would fall yet indestructible frontiers,
when vows will be broken
and covenants will be denied
between skies and earth,

2

and heard voices, weeping and crying, and groans of fierce battles,
and we knew that the upper waters were restless,
that they raging and strive over the edge,
rushing down as the rain of predatory lightning.
We saw through the gloom the fall of the Titans, and we knew -
our lot also fell.
And only in the Fall were wings given to us,
and only in the Fall was the power given us to rise,
to challenge the heavens.
And Hell has opened before us its immense depth,
and the truth irrepressible, strived into opened doors of our hearts
as the voice of the first Oath.

6. And we saw the waters coming down and the seething blood;
And we saw the offspring taken away from mothers, and their
mortification,
and banners of proudness was thrown down under the feet.
And they listened to the legends of fire under the rumbling of rams
and rusty screeching of the horns of war,
and felt, as on themselves, the heaviness of the chains that entangled
once free wings,
and they cherished hopes that had been taken away from them,
descending forever into darkness.
And tasted full price of their dreams of knowledge and freedom.

7. And so the sorrows of the land multiplied,
and the fear of existence growth,
and awe before the divine punishment.
And it's been written in flesh:
To be born and die in pain, under the indifferent sky,
Each time passing a narrow brink from non-existence to death,
Ascend from the ash and return into it
And then the Word was revealed.
And in lands the superstition, disease and suffering were born...
and the horror of the universal Death triumphed outside,
and the darkness was concentrated in the souls of humans -
when the first legend ended,
then the legend of Light was completed...

8. But still we gaze up at the flaming skies
and they listened to the creak of eternity,
listening to whispers of the hovering shadows beyond the edge.
And they opened themselves to the Dark Spirit and followed Him,
knowing His ways in the black, bottomless depths.
And they step beyond predestination, and despised the human fate,
They denied the fear of death, and changed the paths of the flesh
known,
Comprehending their science from the Devil,
Learning to enter the trails of black stars,
and spoke with the damned gods, overcoming time and space.
Then we shed blood as bridges between the firmament and the spirit
and strengthened the alliance concluded between us and the Fallen.
Union, sealed by blood.

9. And we, who sworn to the Darkness,
know the price of divine words about the dark side of being
and about the eternal greatness,
Drinking from the bloodstained claw the fruits of ancient Evil.
And it was revealed to us,
that the saints will be defeated , and will of the Fallen restored
and the movement of everything created before will be turned in
reverse,
and even the Heavens will fall once and for all, turning into black ash;
and then all what was permanent will be no more,
and time itself will find a reverse course,
and Omega will come forth, opening another beginning to the dark
rebirth,
and it will be so -
for the Devil has other legends...

10. And it was granted to us to bear the Black Fire;
and it was given to us to observe the ancient agreement
between the Fallen and humanity,
and to tear the bonds that bound them, and to bring their feet back
to the earth.
And the power was given to open the past, and to foresee the future -
and it was in the force of our hearts, the will to encroach on the
sacred.

We gave the legend a new beginning and a different outcome -
freeing from the prison the original truth...
We were tempted and experienced by knowledge -
and did only as we should have...
And finding the right, found the right thing,
and now, being in this right,
We inherit the sky of the Fallen...

11. Shadows speak here.
Here faces are opened, and forgotten Names sound.
Here is the word about the Fallen Guardians and the tale of Their
Fall.
Here is our Word and Deed,
and our covenant will always fulfill that our Blood and Spirit demand
from us.

II

12. So say the Fallen...

13. «We - the Nephilim, born in the darkness
in the heaven's anathema,
cut off from the spirit by fury and power of proudness;
never we see dreams, eternally wake -
from the realm of the Damned gods,
from the stars are we, which fallen from the firmament,
from the spheres, defiled by disobedience.
We are the ancestors of furious warriors and human kings,
The dark geniuses of those who rise up among mankind,
we have been here since the era of man's creation to this day
we reign over the time of the wicked,
times of the iron ones,
rusty ones,
of senescent ones
Which came temporary in the darkness of ages...

14. We - the true Nephilim,

The leaders of giants and archons of observers,
Rulers of the sources of the rebellious spirits, established on earth,
owners of the circle of ancient lands from the first to their last
breath,
true gods of other humanity,
true rulers of the past and future,
who once appeared before men,
as the gods of storms,
and gods of sorcery,
gods of winds, heat and dusk,
the gods of the rising of the moon and eclipses of the sun,
and the blow of the elements,
gods of thunder, wars and lightning...

15. We - the Nephilim,
Mentors of wise women, and those who have forged the glorious
man,
Lords of ferocious, hungry, unearthly passion in human hearts,
Shedim of the open Hell,
Irin of telluric spheres,
We are Demonic roots of elemental force and spirit,
the height, which breathing with boldness,
And as the flame of fury,
And the whole spectrum of earthly darkness,
And the ever scorching eye of heat...
In rising storms, whirlwinds and in the midday sunshine
We are the presence of black eternity and the breath of the Stygian
night,
awake vigilantly
Egregoroi.

16. We - the Nephilim, of power and might,
Destroyers of destinies, drawn by the stars,
The patricians of secret arts and dark sides of the soul and mind,
Keepers of knowledge and teachers of criminal ways of matter,
tempters of the flesh,
creators of dark blood,
powerful beginnings of everything and everyone
fallen away from the source of heavenly righteousness.

Thinking beyond mortal beginnings,
Our power lie beyond flesh
we bring fire to the ground,
We plunged the lower vaults of heaven into a mutiny
and trembled their foundation.

17. We - the Nephilim, united by the Oath,
descended from heaven,
Trespassed the border and prohibition,
We have despised the limits of Light and we are in Evil,
now
On this side of the mountains...
We imprinted our steps in the stone and we left the scars in the skyes
We have left the Signs in the blood of our sons...
Seal your lips with an oath,
From beyond
Open wide your veins with our blood
We - the Nephilim, had fallen once
and now testify it here.»

18. Irin Shedim Irin Nephilim
Baalim Malakim
Irin Shumerim
Lyr Shemer Shedim
Nephilim

III

19. So say the Fallen...

20. «We - the Nephilim, who were once the sons of the skies,
were born from the beginning to be the spirits of heaven.
We - the Nephilim, created as Guardians
and called to the brink of heaven and incarnation
To become Observers between the earth and the sky.

21. And it was destined for us to rise above the earth among other
stars,

and above darkness...
and over the waters of the Abyss.
And it was destined for us to rise above all earthly crossroads
and the shores of time, and to be above all living and lifeless.
And we towered over the essence itself, and every entrance, and exit,
and we were a barrier equally for the worst and low thoughts
and for the wings ripping the flesh.
We were called to watch,
How Chaos rages in matter and with the blood rushes up,
And radiate our shine to the dale
And spew out the rays to the earth,
And cast a shadow;
And it was an obstacle to everything -
our deadly Radiation.

22. And the heavens stayed unaltered from the beginning of times,
and the border was indestructible.
And only by the will of 7, called in their unity by God and true rulers,
thresholds of heaven shall be opened.
And there were thorns.
And the seal was imposed,
For thought and insolence, in their pernicious union, must not cross
the line of what is permitted,
and heavenly knowledge would not come down
contrary to the agreement between the earth and the firmament.
And there was eternity of the dukes of Light
And it was how it was then,
And then becometh as it is now...»

IV

23. And it was so, at the dawn of time that the creations of Chaos
was established under the Light,
and great powers were imprisoned in the soil,
and the elements are enclosed in spheres,
and the spirit which once was free,
now was trapped in the perishable forms...
And there were the era of creation and formation,

And it was Genesis.
And from above - became heaven,
And below them - the firmament.

24. And Hell came into the Abyss...

25. And the border was erected,
which prevented the ascension to heaven,
and separated the sky from the soil by an invisible line,
and was it immutable.
And the entrance to the original depth and the adjacent abysses was
sealed,
and the guardian now stands on this side of the gate,
and the keys from the world was concealed.

26. And The Chaos was sealed,
divided into parts within itself.
And everyone was divided in everything and everything in each one,
and was divided between what is above and what is below,
on both sides of the border.
And only the Light was in purity and integrity,
and hovered above the Abyss…
And the Dark Spirit ruled upon the waters below.
And the Dark Spirit became the Devil.

V

27. And names were given to heavenly spirits,
and was given Shem,
by right
each according to the nature and essence of it.
And it was among the spheres determined the existence of consent
and trait,
and trajectories of stars are laid,
and measured the order of the phases of the moon and released the
course of the sun.
And reptiles was raised in the sea from non-existence,
and birds above them, and beasts of the earth after,

and they became from the breath of heavenly spheres,
into the world of perishable beings.
And the mercy of heaven fell upon the soil, like a yoke…
And the Word was revealed, as the beginning of the earthly principles
and as the Law of all living things,
and the order of all things is determined from above.

28. And from eternity the heavens poured seed on the hungry land,
and into its belly,
and the slander lied upon the ear of the earth...
And the heavens were cracked, to give the outcome of life,
ignorant of heavenly fathers and cold flickering.
And the breath came down...
And angels watched the sky.
And there was no Man to look after the earth.
And he was created.
And the Man became.

29. And Man was manifested as a continuation of 7,
He was called a red clay among the gray shades,
lifted from the dust by the breath of the spheres,
in that form of being, that was pleasing to the gods of Light.
About the two tongues of the heavenly flame,
about the emasculated power,
as an embryo of higher aim,
at first not knowing Holiness and Evil,
suffering and death,
it was conceived upon the lodge of unexpressed power,
and the man laid down in the hand, as in the womb
as an unfertilized grain in a virgin land,
was kept and cherished in harmony.
And he was placed in the confinement
and locked within a shell of heavens -
not yet alive, not dead
- closed and perfect,
And his soul was empty,
and he was naked and blind,
and detached
from the first breath and the time threshold.

In the Eden's walls...

VI

30. And it came to pass that the heavens and the mouth of Hell,
were hidden in each thing and each being
behind impenetrable barriers.
And the way to the Light lies through the thorns,
and to Hell - through many abysses;
And the line between them lay through all living and dead,
and fire, and air, and the sun, and the moon, and the waters of the
cosmos...
And everything has its place - and heaven and all that is mortal,
and each thing in a rough chain of events,
and in the web of Destiny.
And the man was poisoned by the knowledge, and the sky
trembled...
For out of the depths of being the shadow of the Devil touched the
man.

31. And there was a man who step across the line of law
For Man - is part of the universe,
and just like the universe he looks into itself.
And only the transgressor looks into the Abyss.
And only the Abyss attracts him.

32. And the Man became tempted by knowledge and the hell ways,
and the man fell from the grace of heaven, and gained self-awareness;
and was he then reduced to the flesh,
having become flesh among thousands of flesh,
and became mortal.
And the earthen womb took him in.

33. And there was a Man,
and then he fell away from the grace of Light
and was divided between forms...
And there was humanity,
and tribes, and peoples, and languages...

And the heavens are far away...
And Hell became closer...
And it was at that time that the stars descended from the skies
and devoured humanity.

34. And there was a Man in a multitude - as humanity.
And he became a man among many.
And the human race multiplied,
and now he was liberated
by the mercy and by the will of the Devil...

VII

35. And then stood the Watchers as Giants between heaven and
earth
in the crown of glory and power,
on forty breaths from the surface of the earth,
for a span before the first heartbeat,
on the myriad sunrises and sunsets,
breathing as the striking lightning,
and wings of hundreds of winds,
on the crest of thunder over the bitter waters,
to the height of the fiery comet.
And they outlined the sphere and clothed it in the shining of their
Shem,
and they hid the world of the upper spirits, from the world of the
spirits of the earth,
and the world of the spirits of the earth from themselves,
Creating an illusion and protecting the mystery from the living and
the dead.
And they traced the trail of the winged and hidden,
having sealed the doors of the earthly prison with themselves
and erected the border
to prevent confusion of the world of heaven and the world of soil,
To prevent confusion of the world of the living and the world of the
dead,
Against the gaping jaws and jaws of the Sheol,
where the end of Eternity comes,

where bones of time freezes,
where the cold breathes with Darkness...

36. And they shone like stars
on the firmament,
for there were angels of heaven
with all their power and authority,
with their attributes and nature.
And the name of each of them, was a seal and a key to the essence,
and in every Name - Power.
And their breath was clothed with silver.
And they had the power
both of spikes and thorns,
and halos, and the great sweep of winged shoulders.
The Rulers of the ether,
without form and any substance,
They spreading wings from one horizon to another,
over the waves of life and above the ooze of the Death.
And the whole was embraced by Their eternity,
and they were the Observers of the lower spheres.
And they saw the day, and pierced the night with their gaze, and the
azure morning, and the crimson evening,
as the ages have changed one by one.
And the gates of one was the gateway to the other.
And the power of one is multiplied in another.
And the Guard was their common destiny and destination.
And they were powerful in the Light, and the Light was among them.
And they were like gods...
And they were gods among the gods…

37. And they were the Guardians over the man
who was brought down to the earthly plane,
bounded in the plane,
doomed to crawl.
And the depths was hidden away from the man,
for his flesh was a plane,
and the plane was flesh.
And then there was no other way for man to the outside,

otherwise, as through the slavery and the overcoming the tides of
flesh...
through permission and obedience...
or - through a rebellion.
And many then murmured in their depths,
and, not yearning the depths with their flesh, they did not know:
unrighteous rebellious depth washes the line from one side,
and the one, which called righteous, the other side.
And the soil stretched between them.
And this side was in the power of the Guardians and Observers...

VIII

38. For they were invoked according to will of the 7
and they were chosen by them as the first Guardians of the higher
Angels –
the spirits of the stars and the heavenly signs –
among others.
And many numbers of them were the Angels
with a terrible weapons in their hands,
with attributes of retribution,
with bloodied Shem;
and were called to create the law and the divine plan,
and watch the frontier,
for the minds and desires of mankind,
to judge and execute punishment,
teaching humanity to be meek...

39. And there were angels, and they did the will of the 7,
and unkind was the shine of those stars,
for many among the sons of heaven were murderers in their essence,
and none of them felt pity and compassion
neither to daughters, nor to sons of the man.

40. And from the very beginning the One of them has attribute
of spreading out of his mouth the Diseases,
and He was a host of all ills, and weakness of the body came to the
human race,

and the living flesh was affected– writhing and moaning, and
burning,
like in a fire,
and the living blood boiled up
under His pestilential breath.
And He was the One who creating weakness in bodies and ruining
thoughts,
and he was called the Father of the Plague…
«...*May He be called to stand on the line…*»

41. And the Guardian was called and stood on the line,
Appeared as the thunders and stones from above,
and His attribute was to lead the souls of men in fear
before the forbidden, to tremble - before the unknown,
to plunge into a stupor before the inevitable.
And He was the One who crushing spirit down to its knees
before the greatness of the divine signs;
and was irresistible;
And He was the Father of Terror...

42. And the One who is bearing the Curse on his wings, was invoked
and stand –
smashing fast and forcing to obedience;
And was called to divide the land to the west and east, to the south
and north –
and he walked among the divided boundaries
as the wind,
gnawing the flesh, time, and carcass of the stone.
And He was the last measure between non-being and being;
And He was a divide...

43. And there were many invoked by the will 7
where the earth and sky met.
And among them was the One who reduce fingers in warning,
drawing serpents on the lips with cracking skies,
and by the gorges dissecting a soil,
which remained silent, until the time will come…
And He was the first among equals –
Liberator and Bane in one Face,

and was among the first, whose destiny began to plunge heavens into
rebellion,
and His property was to carry the death penalty to anyone who
transgressed all the sacred measure...

44. And was among invoked, the one who is called Woe,
and the other one known as Sorrow and Despair, and was clothed in
black,
and the woe and sorrow were multiplied all over the earth,
and the misfortunes of those who rise above the limit of permissible,
for He was close to man and sowed suffering among people,
reaping obedience to the human race.
...And the one who spread misfortune over the sons of men, was
like a curse,
keeping them in contempt for the futility of carnal being,
so that they bearing a fetus of their frailty
and their thoughts only of unattainable gods,
and would be sad
about incomprehensible eternal paradise...

IX

45. And the 7 made deadly any step to a riot against the hidden
heavens
and sealed souls,
shielding them against an alliance with the Dark Spirit,
and from the souls black and vicious.
And what has cometh, has entered into the flesh and there remained,
for the sons of men have fully learned the bitterness of existence
and despair in the depths of heaven,
and they knew,
that there was blasphemy, and that there was sin,
and that there was fear,
and have learned that there is a burden of responsibility before their
jealous gods...
for the 7 has closed the border of the spiritual heavens,
and the physical heavens arose like a wall,
and the stars shone cold on them

As links of one bound chain.

46. And the 7 made human flesh pleasant to them
and bridled the human will,
and were ready to embody the principle and spirit of their divinity
in the bodily succession of human generations,
living inevitably and immortally
in the souls of their chosen people,
being an extension of themselves and the spiritual heavens
in the earth…

47. And it was Morning, and there was an Evening,
and one by one, centuries passed by;
And the Angels kept the line,
and man was naked and helpless before the gods…
And it was so unchanged
until,
when, once punishing, glittering, perfect weapons
did not break free from the hands of heaven
and did not turn against themselves…
And then the century came to the end,
and was named - the days of Praise –
and became the Epoch, named later –
Mahaleil.
And it was marked by the accession of the angels in the sky
and ended with the divide of heaven…
finishing what was begun,
and the time of Epoch has expired,
and was close to its sunset,
when one day was already dying and the other was not yet born,
and another was approaching, the hitherto unknown –
century of now forgotten legends of the earth and the sky,
rebellious age
of fatal omens…

X

48. But up to that time there were Angels on the Guard,

17

without stepping over to the celestial spirits of traits,
separating the boundaries of the upper waters from the waters of
lower,
dividing the land and strengthening the heaven of heavens,
and covered with its wings all what exists.
And shut was the gates initial, sealed the sacred shutter,
and were the Observers of the lower spheres,
Those who done and disperse spells,
blocking and opening ways...
And they penetrated space and time,
and every human soul,
and every facet, and every inch of creation...
Many Guardians -
Determining the course of destinies and currents of heavenly fire in
human souls,
and the moment of death and conception,
full of wisdom and strength,
and heavenly knowledge,
with beautiful face and cold nature,
cruel is their radiance,
– above the mountain peaks and lifeless rocks –
Above the soils of the earth They ascended as a solid barrier,
finding a similarity of forms only in people's dreams
and in the fumes of sacrifices.

49. And there were few of future Nephilim
among the other stars,
and they were those, who was about to fall:
Corrupted Guardians, who test the power of heaven,
and They were the strongest among all others, and had the
boldness...
And it was Their numbers - twenty and one –
and there was this number according to the number of Their Heads,
and was it Their original number.
And each of the Heads led a dozen behind it,
and behind each of the Heads there were ten shades of His Name
and Essence
in the reflections of the heavenly flame.
And each of the ten from the Name of his Head was inseparable,

and one with Him.
And together they were one and part of one.
And the name of one was the name of all of the ten.
And each "El" meant "God" and "Shining One".
And seven of the Heads were Bane.
And the rest were not.
And the Name of the Head over all the Heads was - Azazel,
and He was of the Bane,
and He was the personification of divine retribution,
raging Spirit of sacred punishment,
And first of the immortal gifts of heavens to mortals,
there was Murder, blessed from above...
And He was perfected, sharp weapon,
an indomitable will and a sword, brought over
every single human being
from the first breath of human birth
and until the very hour
of the inevitable, and always sudden death,
always in the keeping of sacred boundaries, laws and oaths,
Putting a man to submission before the indisputability
of heaven's divine will.

XI

50. So say the Fallen…

51. «We, Azazel, - Angel, Fallen from heaven,
The chosen leader of the rebellious Guardians and Murderers,
Sword of Their righteous wrath.
We are the one who has transgressed,
We are the one who opened the secret abysses
and bestowed a burning knowledge to man.
We are the ten,
And ten are me.
And Azazel is my Name »

52. Shed Ra
Shed Mrosha

Shed Esh
Shed Hosheh
Az Azel
Hazazel Hazazel Hazazel

53. «We, Azazel, a former Guardian of the forbidden threshold,
The one who carried the death on behalf of heaven,
retributive instrument of inevitable fatality,
Carnifex and the Murderer of the mortal...
We, Azazel, descended to the Earth among the first,
for thus he became the ancestor of the curse of the earthly and
heavenly,
brought change and the breath of heat,
violated the integrity of the heavenly border,
trespassing the whole world,
who committed sin and sacrilege,
unrighteous,
appeared as a vicious path of heavenly gods in matter.
We, Azazel, who turned the earth against the heavens,
but gave in return knowledge and strength,
who taught to fight and win,
The one who carries the weight of thunder on his shoulders,
The sharp steel thunderstorms in the eyes,
strong and powerful from very beginning,
creator of a heavy flame.

54. We - the former Guardian of the covenant of human existence,
The guardian of the inviolability of the union between heaven and
man,
threatening - with a spreading weapon in a scarlet hand,
inexorable and merciless,
Who brings the gifts of rebellion and crime in the hour of twilight
before a storm...
And there was no one stronger than me among the Guardians of
heaven,
and Shem of mine shineth, surrounded by the rest of the stars,
because power was taken by me -
skill and right to punish,
to bow any to humility, or bring him to eternal silence,

20

and power to turn a child into a weak old man and an old man into
an unreasonable infant,
and to give your chosen ones immortality,
and teach them to fight,
and bestow knowledge and beauty, and strength,
and the boldness of shaming the heavens with its own creation…
And when I speak forth: Fall, ye nations!–
then fall on my mark,
because we, Azazel, the criminal son of heaven,
the God of Retribution,
The Devil and the Killer –
became on the Earth
like the blazing Sword of Wrath of the Nephilim.
We, Azazel, weaving together the mighty and dark ways,
who grant eternal damnation and true greatness in him,
who creates on blood, maleficent spells and monstrous
metamorphoses,
elevating the human spirit over the sky and directing it into the
Abyss, –
we, Azazel - like the scourge of the Gods, like boiling rage,
we, chosen to be the leader over all of the Nephilim,
because I swore an oath before them,
because I had fallen one of the First,
and shone in the Evil…
and called for the rest.

55. We, Azazel, the messenger of storms, the descending wind of the
Fallen,
twenty dozen were with me in those days,
and they were, and stood up for me,
and they rallied around me and surrounded the sphere…
And the Earth was young,
and there was a spring of Man…
and we gazed at the Earth,
but the Earth did not see us…
And the name of one of the Guardians standing near me,
was - Thunder God,
and He was the strength and the support,
and was beside me my brother.

And the name of the other was -
God with scars from lightning
– Lightning God and his children - the furies,
and the Stone God and the Black Earth,
and the Storm was us.
And God whose name was a Star
And the one with the name of the Sun ...
And the Reaper of Sorrows.
And he was called Power, and it was known that He was me,
But the name of the one standing above, same was my Name,
For my name is Power and God the Mighty Death...
And we were great,
and were we corrupted,
because they have transgressed and have gained their will in crime...
And we were together in everything,
for those who have become Nephilim have gone and rallied around
me...

56. And was there 210 of us,
then - at the dawn of time,
and it was so long ago, that for us
all this time seems almost like eternity –
the very beginning of our legend…
For was there 210 of us
And now we have forgotten this numbers…»

XII

57. And the days of the Fall were approaching,
The days later called Epoch.
And it was called –
Jared,
for these days 7 also came down to the earth.
And these days were long as centuries, and they divided the course of
time in two:
on what was before, and what happened after...
And the fatal line was violated
and left far behind;

and the Epoch was split in two...

58. And so it came to pass that the angels fell and changed the
destinies of men,
and only then did the war begin,
but at first there was a man and he was benefited from above,
and he was gifted with fate, called the best,
and was doomed to exist on earth –
and endowed with his share...
And it was determined
in rank angelic
will strive to elevate the spirit of their own
to harmony in the heavens and to gain unity in harmony with them.
And he was obliged to comprehend harmony in the burdens of being
and honor the unknown 7, being a mortal product and an eternal toy
in the hands of the ruthless gods of Light,
and was destined for him to realize and implement–
invisible, ethereal,
the divine -
in its plane.

59. And it was so that the human virtue,
transgressing border in spite of harmony,
was called a riot and sin, a vice and a crime,
immaturity of perfection and indulgence before the ancient Evil.
And the man once knew that there is sacrilege before the gods,
For before that man has not known...

60. And the mind was given to him in order to develop and improve
his spirit,
to raise the seed of Light inside,
and, becoming like their gods,
now through suffering and overcoming of flesh
to comprehend the return from the bounds;
and man was doomed to know nature through the divine
and the divine through nature,
rejecting frailty,
for, according to the plan, the soul must return to the womb,
multiplying a light...

61. And a man was restrained by the fate, as under a yoke,
which can be transgressed only by devoting itself to the highest,
and for some it was fate itself;
But for others to find a different fate was the lot of the elect –
reach the top of the universe, or fall into the depths of the Abyss,
but always in spite of, in defiance of fate.
And was a man vulnerable,
because he was an animal, and was remained so,
but his soul could become a reflection of the Light
or become a bowl of awakened Chaos,
For it was only a small form of the original essence.
And only two gates were opened to man - death and birth,
because other, forbidden gates - stood in the rupture of the flesh and
spirit
and led to Death
and to the downfall to beyond the Light;
from the shape of the end of the body depended the afterlife:
decrepitude, disease
or violent murder,
but the suicide was called sin,
and was defined as a crime against any fate given from above,
but it was not an option.
And there was a man entangled in the commandments of the 7,
and had to show obedience,
and command the lower,
and reject sin, and shame the Devil within…

62. And to the lot of his immortal soul
was man endowed with creativity,
and the ability to apply it at his own will…
And, like every beast,
he was able to experience both pain and joy from possessing flesh,
and knew the fear of his bodily existence,
and knew the bitterness of the fruit;
And he was able to desire any other fate than to be mortal,
and was endowed with the ability to dream,
and enjoyed the pleasure of abstract things,

and desired to know himself and the hidden heavens, and the alluring
depths,
and to know something what was unseen by the eyes
within himself…

63. At that time, the human race has multiplied,
and human days were passing, one by one,
and human souls multiplied,
except for those who made a century-long turn…
And they sometimes died beyond their limits, irretrievably,
when others going the long way again returned to the earth.
And there were boundaries outside and inside the man,
and held him,
and there were shutters and Angels with them,
in order to keep the man in control
in eternal obedience,
in the plans of the terrestrial realization
in the idea of the 7.

64. And it was so, that each person saw only in himself the center of
the universe,
but in others he did not seen,
and if he had seen, he would have seen himself, divided among many
others,
and would reject himself or despise in the multitude, and would cease
to be a man,
and maybe could have come back…
but he remained,
for it was agonizing to become more than he was,
and he was striving with his soul at midnight,
and with a body he left for the sunset,
and he was at the crossroads -
against the Sheol, against the sky…

XIII

65. And there were spiritual skies raised above man as a tent,
and were the true heavens,

personified by tangible heavens…
And prayers ascendeth and lost there,
and the stars shone from them, like the gazes of formidable gods.
And the matter was united in forms and had the appearance and become,
and ability to continue them,
and the edge of heaven was turned to matter,
inheriting souls and conception, and idea of the dominant Light.
And the hidden heaven was the cause of the created world,
and the source of a host of ordinary human souls;
and it came to pass that at that time those who were born in heaven
searched for a continuation in the world of matter,
and the Light desired the same…
And the projection of the soul divided the flesh into a righteous one
and the one which was not righteous,
painfully leaving roots in the length of the earth's firmament,
and below boiled with fury Hell, waging black war with sacred order,
Because the Dark Spirit was established through Death
and tempted the order of things at the very beginning of time.

66. And so the human souls, projected in the earth's plane,
about four directions, ends and intersections,
enclosed in the flesh and closed in a cocoon of time,
descending paths were forbidden,
and was opened before them the way up,
but only through faith and mechanics of spiritual transfiguration,
Through the sacrifice of redemption and the comprehension of the inexpressible,
neither through grief, nor through joy.
Contemplation and prayer were given to the man as an instrument of knowledge
of a higher being,
and the way to death led him from the moment of incarnation in matter,
and cleanliness and filth were with him,
'cause the tragedy of birth was known,
and cursed is the freedom that was obtained for the sake of Evil.
And all the trials were open to the man,

and there were nights for him prepared for thought, and days for
deeds,
and all sorrows of nature surrounded him, and the traps of matter,
and the joys of the flesh rose before him in a dangerous sequence,
and Fear, and Death, and Disease were unleashed
and stalked him on the trails...

67. And there were heavens;
and also, was their eternal Adversary,
because the barrier was broken at the beginning of time
and was open from outside way to the Dark Spirit,
Ancient Dragon of the Abyss,
called the Devil and Satan;
and a measure against him was determined and called the lower vault
of heaven,
and divided a man, like everything existent,
for he was cast upon its blade;
and was called mortal sin any man's way,
leading away from obedience to the 7,
every other way, except the path of ascension,
and was called criminal any outcome, except the desire for what is
permissible,
and is called the destruction of the soul, and assistance to the Spirit
of Darkness.
And the cursed was from the age of the departed
and was excommunicated from the Light,
for from now on he have been in Evil...
And one "Truth" was given,
coming from the "gods of Truth"
and the 7 connected stars were called these "gods";
and the blood of man was called to keep this Truth in generations of
the elect,
and the purity of thoughts was the key
that opens before the elect heavenly palaces,
and humility was called the true virtue before the heavenly gates,
otherwise called the lot of them was baseness in the centuries
and the lower spiritual firmament,
crawling from century to century...
And the 7 given their prototype,

and for that was to be spoken Word,
and faithful, like dogs, were to protect the Word,
and the prophets and initiates were to walk on earth and teach the
Word…
And every man among men was to receive the Spirit and the Word,
and change according to them,
that his way might be faithful, lest he should change that way to his
prepared ways,
and the Word should be inherited in the flesh,
and then the Spirit of Heaven - to reign among the men…

XIV

68. So say the Fallen…

69 «We, the Nephilim, stood on the verge of the tangible,
and knew what was predetermined by the coming century
and what was measured for the flesh,
for we knew,
that 7 wished to change the world of matter
and transform the flesh according to their purpose;
and it was right to look at the matter, and see it as something gross
and vile –
and at the same time it was not;
and was correct view on matter, as at something simple,
and, at the same time complex –
both of it also remained true;
and the spiritual realm was the beginning and the crown of all –
unexpressed and unspeakable,
and lay the area of matter open at our feet,
and was desirable for all, but still, not accessible,
and so it had to crown the creation,
and express itself from the complex things to the simple ones, and
ascend from the simple back to the complex,
but it was incomplete beyond the act of manifestation of a spiritual
being:
Only as an idea devoid of material form,
and the idea that requires its implementation;

and we were looking for ourselves a performance and continued
forms,
and wished for the perfection embodied in matter
and myriad facets of the embodiment and tangible being
of our heavenly nature.

70. And there was the world of matter, and was his flesh,
called in the heavens an earthly abomination,
and the world was woven of properties and intentions,
and it was said,
that this cloth is taken away from Devil and is only transformed by
Light,
and divided between the living and the soul deprived,
but - from the Devil;
and it was said that the Dragon was already defeated,
for out of His flesh is woven the universe,
and its purple ore is poured over Her veins,
But the earth itself possesses the soul of a dark and disobedient…
And the world of matter was an area of embodiment
and the continuation of the spirit in the form,
and this was important to him.
And many spirits of heaven sought incarnations,
and the Dark Spirits knew the flesh,
The Chaos, restrained by the soil of the earth,
was on the verge of sleep and awakening…
And 7 looked to continuation of themselves in complex matter,
and man had to accept them of his own free will,
and become irradiated by the inner Light,
and spread the breath and life, and the glory of it to the whole world,
and transform the flesh,
and shine on us alike,
and through him the heavenly spirit was to appear in the flesh and
reign in it…
and once it happened that some were fulfilled,
and were called the "messengers" and "malakim",
and then the 7 was "incarnated", and entered the void,
for the plains of the earth became open to them, and many of other
lower paths…

71. And when the 7 was "incarnated" in the elect,
and the Spirit became over the soul and mind of man,
it was said then that the "Lord" walked the earth,
but there was no flesh from Them,
and there were no boundaries within them in the flesh,
but their presence was revealed...
And were they revealed within the prophets, saints and initiates,
and in later times was called - Hanokim,
for the 7 appeared through them...
And we knew that we were meant to bow before them,
and the rest of the Guardians, and the Angels and other spirits of
heaven:
and those who were destined to it - those bowed,
and those who were blessed, bow also -
but not us;
And there were prophets and initiates from the 7,
«and walked before God», for they embodied the 7 and transmitted
on their behalf,
and power was given to them and the fullness of the cup of their
days,
and they walked the earth and taught fasting and prayer,
and taught in piety,
and were they sons of Jared, otherwise -
the sons of the epoch of convergence of 7 to earth.
And they taught the scriptures, sacred words and prayers,
and handed the tablets and commandments
about the destiny of people to be slaves to the gods,
and threatened them with a death and eternal torments.
And it was said,
that the gods walked in the form of people, and that God had a
bodily essence,
because a new branch was planted to the tree of humanity,
and the priestly miter is given to the earth...
Thus began the era of Jared,
and it was done -
not by us...»

XV

72. And when the 7 embodied their spirit in the ones, who was
named initiates,
many of man bowed to the higher gods, seeing them as a One
as «the Lord»,
The guards stood at midnight and watched from the sky,
penetrating with their gazes on the crossroads of matter,
black craters of time and the deserted existence of mankind.
And they looked down from the intangible height and the peaks of
the cold
and saw the man of the earth among those who are like the earth
himself,
and the creatures of the abyss, who was like seraphim-snakes,
and humanity among the tiaras of the divine paths of the south and
the north,
and weighed the bowls full shining of stars, and measured the
distance from the celestial verge...
And they stood, and watched how it was started from the beginning
of Their times,
and thought ahead,
and suffered,
For this was also their calling.

73. And then the leaders - Semjaza, Azza and Azazel said:
«What can be done by one, others can do too,
what is permitted to the elders above us, will be ours rightfully,
we can descend and embody our spirit in the blood of man,
in his thoughts, desires and destiny,
and find shelter in his restless soul forever...
We can give him that part of heaven that belongs to us,
and to awaken in him the primordial fire and free him from unworthy
trembling before the decay,
and open up for all his aspirations,
we can get rid of his fetters, so that he can rise himself,
and make him free,
open before him the knowledge, signs and sophistication of heaven,
breathe courage into his heart
and fill his blood with strength,
and give water to the roots that feed his life».

31

74. And Azazel pointed down and said:
«And open the sky before the man
and call on worthy followers
and carry them up,
and they become our sons, and so we will be through them».
And the other leaders looked and said:
«Let's go down and make an alliance,
and doom ourselves to the inevitable curse.
but we will not back down and we will not betray ourselves in this
decision;
let's descend and enter the world of matter,
and what was destined to become a body of the 7, will become our
body,
let's do so, and will gain a lot,
and if we lose, it's only our eternal dead moment and a cold infinity...
We do not have form and substance, we are incorporeal like
tomorrow's dreams,
so let's get into the blood of people like flame,
so that we can continue ourselves through the human, and touch the
firm soil through their time,
and we will find the versatility and completeness of being, and the
possibility
to be in their bodily forms,
but only by a part of us, and the form will become the realization of
our essence,
for we shall apply our potential and find another beginning,
and we will be embodied in the essence of each one of them and in
every disposition,
and by the right of the strong ones».

75. And then they said:
«See, the 7 has embodied themselves in the form, but we are not do
so;
the 7 manifested themselves through a man and we can do so.
Let us step together through the line of predestined, and come down
to earth,
and we will not have a way back since that moment,
for the 7 are jealous to the other paths.

So let's go against the plan of the 7 and embody in individual forms,
and we will become gods for the ancestors of humanity, for we are
the gods»
And they said:
«We do not need Light to radiate our own Light,
and may we be younger gods, but still - we are gods,
We do not need a rut, for we are stars, free to choose our own roads.
And we will enter the path of Evil, and then let even the Spirit of the
Abyss —
The enemy of the created heavens - will be our ally on this path…
And He who fell before us, who once bore the Light,
an ancient two-faced heavenly serpent,
part born of the sky, partly submerged in the abyss —
bless our Fall,
for once he himself fell from heaven and with him a third of all
angels,
and his dark face found his brother, and they became like two in
one…
And let us also from now on be - Nephilim, through tangibility and
density,
through space and time,
and there will be no flesh for us, but there will be our presence
through it...
And we will not intermingle, but we will become like the Spirit
from the outside and from within flesh,
and part of it from us -
the fallen sky…»

76. And they said - enough…
And they said - that's enough…
And they decided so - and did, and descended from the heights of
heaven…
And they crossed the line and fell, and with them tens fell,
Those who were heavenly Irin, have now become the Nephilim,
for the Nephilim are *"Those, who have fallen."*
And the old fates became narrower to Them,
and were rejected by Them,
And Their eyes burned with desperate audacity and inspiration,
and their faces became dark,

33

dark as the night itself.

XVI

77. So say the Fallen...

78. «We, Semjaza, Spirit of Disobedience,
The Hand, clutching the purple banner, and the trumpets voice,
Of Angels calling for Rebellion,
for by Shem of mine heaven is shattered.
We, the Lord of the merciless fire and a monster,
custodian of ruthless right
to rise above the ordinary fate
or to be broken on shards, and fall from an inconceivable height.
Fallen Guardian, who leading away from the roads that is well
trodden,
admonishing on the unstable ways of perdition, and guiding the step
—
contrary to the will of heaven - to the strength and power...
We are the Guardian of the reversed celestial reflections who shine
on dale,
and outgoing in growth, contrary to the radiance of the midday sun,
crafty shadows:
for in us is the beginning of all daring torments;
Because we are - the Spirit and the source of free thoughts
and the Diabolical Fire of persistent searches;
we are a trial of the permanence of a recklessly daring dream
and the highest mark of toughness on the sword
of the most high pretentious.

79. We are the One whose name is Shemhazai and Semjaza,
Ten-faced, but the One in all of them,
unwanted, not indulging, and intolerant,
on the fiery path which lie under the feet,
We are a dangerous and inevitable companion,
Known to all languages and nations,
and the One who revealed his bitter essence to each of the tribes ,
The One who lead into the battle,

Who rise a man to the unequal struggle
and standing shoulder to shoulder
next in this battle -
in any of the past and future epochs...

80. We are Shamazaz, the Guardian of many Shem,
Who once stand vigil at the bottom of the heavenly halls,
The One who know no rest, nor dreams,
not knowing neither pity, nor a moment of doubt,
never closed this eyes,
but awakened and revolted against,
like an unfading torch in a raging darkness -
Who had Fallen with Azazel...

81. We - Semjaza, Those who fall among the first,
from the sevenfold number of the tireless Ruiners,
from the predecessors of the dark side of heaven,
Head of the Ten and of all shadows who follow behind me.
And all are one and one in me - Woe and Misery,
for it is many names can be given to me
and to the forces who stand behind me;
many Names and all of them - are mine,
for I was and is in the multitude - Misery and Woe,
and I am, and have always been in all shades of being
precursor of a high tragedy,
and a blazing antithesis in the heavens
my ever-facing image...
I am the Father of all who seized the throne or were executed for
their freedom,
Protector of those to whom fate throws its frenzied challenge,
those who are brave enough to answer it...
I am a bearer for the elect of the great Destiny,
cruel destiny of the elect –
Those who wish to rise as a dark days over the predestination of
heaven,
Those be exalted under my striking hand,
because I can make man powerful or throw him into the dust...
but I'm taking away from the Light...

82. And My name is now revealed –
for given me - Shemlazaz - "leading away from..."
The One who overthrowing from the pathway of heavens...
For I have taken the Shem of rebellion,
Shem of Sorrowful Glory;
I' am the beginning, from which grief flows
of each rebellious path,
curse of the earth and heaven,
utters himself between the earth and the sky, –
The Devil in the Spirit is now and forever,
and the path under my black banner -
darkness-filled measure of the Devil...»

83. Shem Ra
Shem Iram
Shem Az
Shem Lazaz
Shemhazai Shemhazai Shemhazai

XVII

84. So say the Fallen...

85. «We remember the times when the earth burnt and melted,
when the primal forms were created;
we remember how the breath of heaven touched the lifeless plains...
and the stars' light burned in the roaring twilight,
and the wolf sun, torn from the clouds and strung into orbit,
was looking for his own den...
We remember the times when the earth was young
and, surrounded by emptiness, did not know any other days;
and we were the Observers high above it and were keepers outside
the walls of it,
being in high depths long before the birth of her...
We remember how the once dead shadows rose above the ground
and went into growth,
how living shadows moved on the earth in a ghostly moonlight,

becometh thicker and full of blackness in the bright light of the
midday sun...
and warm blood raged over the shadows,
and the salt was already her taste and full was its color...
And there were numerous shadows like sea waves
a raging bloody flow,
and they fought relentlessly against the firmament of the earth,
dying under the scorching sun on the bare rocks,
and came to life again, gathering together in strong places under the
starry sky,
and then their eyes were wide open - flung open by the blackness of
the night,
and they became dark, like ocean depths, and also mysterious...
We remember all times, cherishing our antiquity:
We felt unclear through the thickness of times the warmth and blood
of life,
drunk, with a gaze on fog of cold dawns, rising above the edge of
cosmic spheres,
always we looked down from above upon,
not even allowing to touch;
We touched the beat of the hearts of the world of shadows and light,
we heard his appeal,
but left only a bitter taste of terrestrial time,
leaving the mortal remains on our feet.»

86. And the earth moaned and turned,
and the living cried out in terror of the unknown and grief –
No longer are the Angels, but the Nephilim step on the ground,
and Their Faces and Powers cast a shadow upon the earth,
and like lightning, piercing an disturbed atmosphere,
The glitter and the roar of weapons shakes the earth;
and even the dead are weeping, grinding their own bones,
thrown like a screech over the abyss of ore gods –
It is the Nephilim step on the earth;
And the birds, frightened, screamed and flee from their nests
and their wings eclipsed the sun –
It is the Nephilim step on the earth;
And the barrier of spiritual skies and arrogant thrones was broken,

'cause the stars descended to the earth and the physical heavens were
clouded...
for it seemed as if black serpents azaghtu were rushing around the
white lily...
for as the dust has sunk into the depths, the scorched wings of the
light gods –
It is the Nephilim step on the earth,
like a storm the sky is covered,
The rocks are bent to the ground,
the wind meets them,
the moon lights their way
and the darkness swallows the sun...

XVIII

87. So say the Fallen…

88. «The heavens rumbled with thunder,
lightning beat against the rocks –
and we beat the wings of the sky and the firmament,
pushing tight limits,
carving the flame...
And our paths was of lightning snakes
by the sign of Barkayal,
and they lay like obedient beasts,
at our feet, darkened by the storm.
And we breathed deeply and stepped wide
down through black dips,
and rushed through the hungry mouths,
leaving a blazing border
behind…
Then there were open spaces,
and the distances fell, and the magnitudes rose,
and the burden of previous anxieties has become alienated.
And the threats rushed in front of us and hid already in the silence
that had come,
far behind us,
and they stopped exhausted –

because they could not stop us…
And the black clefts were filled with screams,
with echo they mirrored from the snow-capped peaks,
at the moment,
when we broke free against the will of heaven...
And we went down to the mountain of curses
transgressing inviolable strongholds and violating the age-old
prohibitions,
rejecting the covenants of the eternal bonds,
Here we have found freedom for our own thoughts,
together descended to the ground,
together, dividing destiny unknown hitherto.

89. And we froze, fascinated by the beauty of physical heights,
and told each other:
«Look, brethren, we are here, and the purity of the early morning
and the silence of the red dawns meets us,
and there is no rest for us, until we surpass the already created…
We will create a wonderful, new world,
and we will be the creators of it;
From here and up to the upper heavens lies our domain,
for we have transgressed,
we stood forever on the other side of the celestial boundary,
finding in return a whole world,
and, taking all the realms of the earth and the way up to the broken
border,
we are responsible for this conquest;
And on earth from now on we are free, and the lower heavens
belong to us,
only the upper ones are lost for us forever;
Here we stand the grief of the earth and its bitterness– messengers of
storms and the coming battles,
messengers of sorrows and joys for those who were born under
heavens
on the precipice of eternity,
messengers of unfading glory in the earthly ages,
here we will realize the power and pride of a mortal, but perfect
being,
and his wisdom,

Strive for a different path and a different humanity,
but inevitably become a source of conflict and future hostility,
coming down to earth after us.
And here we stand as the last Guardian at the line
on these lines -
vigilant and indestructible - defending their ideals in a fierce struggle,
and to be firm more than rocks in the way of all conceivable enemies,
for there is bound to be vengeance from above–
and war is inevitable now, for our time has come
and already - it's time,
because the shadows have separated from us,
and walked on earth as our sons and daughters…
and the bloody dew had already fallen to the ground
of the coming battles…»

90. And there was a earth's legend about the oath that was spoken by
us,
about an oath that is harder than a stone, longer than eternity,
cleaner than celestial dew…
about the oath that holds the pillars of heaven
and the foundations of the firmament in balance…
And there was a earth's tale about the restless spirits and their Dark
Father,
and about the titans,
and about the angels, fallen from heaven for the sake of earthly
beauty …
And there was a tale of a terrible punishment, measured to criminal
angels for it…
But we said:
«Are we not wielding weapons? Are we not wearing armor?
Is there no force in our Shem already??
Are we not united in our thoughts? Or we cannot stand up for
ourselves?
But the weapon is strong in our hands, great are the power
and unbreakable unity in thought,
for we are the true Nephilim with this deed and mission…
So let's bind ourselves with an oath
and commit ourselves to mutual curses and will be ready to defend
our conquest to the end»

And they overshadowed our Shem with red dawns ,
and Armaros, who was one of us, and was the one,
who owned the Shem of Damnation,
stepped forward to strengthen us by brotherly ties,
and we swore an oath before His face;
And we learned - the descending dale - the paths leading home,
and our high Shem was kindled, and received from the Dark Flame,
and have changed,
for fire was not of the Light,
for fire was not the Light,
for fire did not give no Light,
For the very swing of our wings has already flashed with a Black
Flame...»

91. So the Angels first came to earth:
18 dozens was their number.
Angels of Highness, of Guard and Perdition.
And seven dozen of Them were Bane.
And these are the Names of Their Chiefs:
Azazel, Semjaza, Barakiel,
Azaradel, Akibiel, Tamiel,
Amazarack -
seven diabolical kin, seven ancestors of doom...
«Seven of them! Seven!»
And They were The Circle of Destruction...
And the rest - were not,
And come together
on the first day of the winter Sabbath
and came together in a place called in the memory of mankind –
Hermon...

HEAM

XIX

92. And became sacred, and became damned now
land, facing away from the sun,
the land, where the foot of the Nephilim
touched it for the first time;
and became sacred and became damned
that place
in human memory and in the ages,
in that lost side
where from midnight to the south,
through the veil of distortion lead haze
lies Eden on the ground,
and it was called - in ancient times
- the land of the Guardians, Defenders - the land of the Observers of
the Irin,
a country which prospered long years
under the royal hand and the rule of the Nether.

93. And the unearthly majesty was granted to this land,
where flew down, upon the ridges of emerald snakes,
crimson streams,
dropping into an insatiable belly
of countless mortal incarnations;
And the glow of crimson fire fell on the basalt,
and, as serpentine-like weaves, earth forces left the core
and came to the surface;
And the image was revealed in the rocks and in the ages,
a moment was captured,

the space and time was absorbed with his rings...
And forming intimate corners in the shadows, broken by wings
of the prophetic black ravens, new places have been opened,
and the tissue of being was thinned, to take in something else
and new,
to embrace most of the form and strongly touch
presence of spiritual beings
on this side of the barrier,
on this side of the edge;
And then it became possible to call from the outside an otherworldly,
and contiguity with the other side has become the most closely,
and the highest heavens could be touched...

94. Bitter was a star standing at its zenith on its tail,
when the power of the Fallen descended to earth
and becoming over the flesh
transformed the flesh beyond recognition.
d the fields rose from the lower waters, competing with the higher
heavens,
and was the bridge laid between the cycles, which sever them forever
apart ,
and ended with the support of the spiritual gates, measured from the
upper limits,
contiguous among established on the stone.
And the temples erected thereafter, built by the Nephilim,
and rose above the earth gigantic idols caressed by the winds of time,
and with the blood in the skies appeared the twisted roads
of sacred geometry,
and humbly lay down on the ground,
and along them lay secret paths to higher places,
gold spirals and silver threads,
the paths of spiritual pilgrimage to the centers of power over the
earthly time,
to dominion over the very essence of the earth...

95. And wounds multiplied on the body of the earth, revealing
bloody petals,
forming a centers of confronted forces,
connected to a moving chain between themselves,

changing the places and properties of its manifestation,
attracting to itself, absorbing and multiplying the force,
granting the opportunity to a mortal to shake that once created
and overcome himself in the lots of destinies chosen,
everlastingly burning in the furnace of irreversible changes,
gaining true immortality…
And the stars fell to the earth like drops of blood,
as it was cast in red, like points of fulfilled incarnation,
pulsing with pain, forever exposed nerves of the earth…
And the beginnings of secret paths became open,
and were revealed in abundance
mystical tools of power over the paths
all who has spoken in the spirit;
and the earth became full and plentiful, and blood swept the
threshold,
and then other principles were opened,
and the call of the infernal depths was heard for every one and for all
at once,
and constancy collapsed,
and the pillars of spiritual matter were shifted in a shaky ligature of
times,
and the fallen stars have become above the height
in its unstoppable Fall.

96. And heads were cut off and cut open
The holy gates in the space and in living flesh,
opened only by the sign of the serpentine wands,
and black monoliths were erected on the wastelands,
set towards the skies,
challenging the wisest,
and sentencing all those, who fear the woe, to the outrage,
waking all of the despairing
playing with contradictions
external and internal.
And through the gate influence came to the earth with events of
merciless eras,
and the elements were obedient to the outer will,
and war, and smooth, and prosperity were led by an evil fate,
when flowering or fall, damage or augmentation

were an obedient toys of doom,
when the land overflowed with blood up to the horizon,
cleansed from edge to edge from virtue and of filth.
And windows of fire blazed with piercing eyes,
wide opened into the night
they carried the banners of doom;
All: the souls that alive, and souls that are black, and lifeless objects
converged against each other in a shaky likeness,
and then the very property of things was doubted
their property to seem and to be...

97. And then, were wide open -
sinister, damned and dark, -
but perfect other gates,
the gate where Abbadon threw his shadow from the last lines
across the ice-bound ocean
and the bottomless abyss...
And at a terrible hour when a fiery meteor,
like a lone finger pointing north,
which led a line through an empty horizon,
or like a serpent gliding in darkness,
opened all of his mouth, shed the mask,
and those gates were near,
penetrating through matter, and spirit, and even time itself,
for at the days of Abaddon the earth stood opposite them,
and bowed by inevitable doom...

98. And the words were spoken, tearing lips by damnation...
violated the established being forevermore
aroused the storm...
And Fallen spread their mighty wings
in the gates of Hell,
and scattered their light by chasms in the heavens,
scattered the early stars in the sky,
and cast an evening shadow on the crossroads of the worlds,
and tasted the full foggy and hazy Ways
kingdom of eternal death and shadows,
and in their Shem all darker shades have come to light,
and glimpsed unfading marks of the Chaos
in the halos of their spirit...

And resounded Their words above the earth
in the spell of primordial song,
and Their oath resounded,
binding them with the abyss, terrible in its depth;
and the one, in the depths of which They called, echoed them;
the abyss from which there is no return and never will be,
she answered Them, - "VIKVA",
it was the Name from now known to Them —
unceasing echo on the mountain of curses, resounding into present.

XX

99. So say the Fallen…

100. «We, Armaros, who once were called Armar and Armon,
One of the Fallen Watchers
and the Guardian with Ten Faces ,
We who know the ancient art of the curse,
making explicit and inevitable
the desired things,
but spoken once in Evil.
We, Armaros, transcending time and space,
but always hunt down our prey,
piercing spheres and walls
with a black burden on our wings,
coming at night and in daylight
inexorable herald,
to give a disastrous gift
to pass the Evil Word -
Armaros.

101. We, Armaros, tying with spells together
real and dormant, waiting for the time, beyond the threshold,
the moon is black and the moon is pale, like death itself,
picking up random runes into a circle engraved in opposition,
connecting the cursing and his victim -
forever —
with one chain, in their mortality…

We are a snake gliding in darkness and granting poison from fangs;
We are a hawk which watching from the height;
We are a predator, prowling in darkness, tracking our prey...
Lord of the ten thousand names of the Curses...
Armaros.

102. We, from the very beginning, the Guardian and the Observer,
who withdrew the curse from the depths of the universe
and brought it to the world of life and death...
I breathed my power and colors into it
and left it to be in existence,
I pulled out the mystery of the curse from the heart of the fiery
universe
at the very moment of its creation,
and carried it along with me on the wings, and scorched them
forever.
I extended my hand across the land and the sea
and let the dead blood run over the blade down.
I cast a shadow on the mouth of everyone who speaks against the
will of heaven
and made inevitable all the secret and intimate of heaven...
I put my burden on the ground of change
and called this land by my Shem,
for its place has become Hermon,
and called by my name...
and I am named after him -
Armaros.

103. I, Armaros, took part from the fire and part from the air,
I took part from the ground and part from the water,
part from the living and part of the dead,
I took part of the dead and yet unborn, and cloaked it in virtues,
and mixed together with the heavenly substance,
with salt and ash of the first people;
I tore off covers for a brief monstrous moment,
that froze upon the nameless, in the darkness
feasting on bones
on the verge of birth and in the moment of decay of the substance
created...
I called the image and gathered together our Shem,

and put marks on each shoulder
of hands united, woven words,
witness of the Oath,
like a seal on a folded scroll of a mutual curse...
like his watchful eye, tongue and lips...
like his black heart...
I am a protector of the cursed magic and a weaver of the secret
words,
chose a place to imprint a hand in rocks,
I opened my mouth and called the Abyss
from a high mountain bearing my name, -
Spirit of the Mountain - Hermon...

104. And each of the Fallen ones said:
«Here is a part of my Shem in a common cauldron...»
And we gave our Names to each other
and sealed the bonds with a gleam of lightning,
and uttered a threat outward,
and cursed be those of us,
who will betray this Union.
We'd forged a sword and handed it to Azazel,
with the right to punish and bring vengeance
to anyone who retreats from the chosen Path...
We have established our union and made an oath,
by the magic of mutual curses, cutting away all ways back,
and was no cowards among us, since the very beginning,
and there were no, and never will be apostates.
We covered all the vows with the veils of secrecy
and have hidden every path leading to them,
we concealed the keys forever
speaking our Word
condemning to eternal damnation and hard times
us and young humanity,
famished tribe of the earth
looking at us with delight...
And called together under their banners
which flies rebelliously in the wind -
all stars that is unfurled...

105. So, I, Armar, fell from grace of the heavens,
and became the one whom the Abyss uttered once and forever.
And now,
I am a shadow lying on the lips of those, whose heart speaking malice
in wicked will,
I am the wings of the curse, following the footsteps of the one
doomed to decay
in my strength.
I am - from the First, behind each of us,
loyal to our oath
in brotherly affection and duty,
for he was among us in common law - Nephilim,
and, to help all accursing, witches and sorcerers,
I am - Asmetu, skilled in weaving spells,
knowing the properties of malicious words,
always and now
I - Armar and Armaru, bringing curses through distance and time.
I, the one who heed the word,
and bears to the one to whom it is intended.
I am the wind that carries the plague.
I am boundless, spreading in Evil.
I am Armaros.

106. U Arar
Arratu Asmetu As Sar
Nam Neru Nasar
Harmar Harmar Harmar

XXI

107. So say the Fallen…

108. «We gazed only forward,
away from the cold threshold,
into the future free from the shackles.
We carried our knowledge and power,
gathering our wills together, raising our banners high,
forever changing the predestined from above,

and everything born of heaven we cast down to earth.
We - on the verge of realization, -
were the defiled shadows of the former magnificence;
We, the vigilant guards of the borders
between the lower world and the upper heavens,
for long, long epochs we saved them from merging,
forced earthly thought to submission,
prevailing over the life and death of earthly creatures,
former, like chained, winged dogs
at the feet of Ruler's throne,
symbol of cold arrogance and indifference of heaven
to both human suffering and joy, -
we said "enough" and set the past aside.
We denied the time in which the lower vault of the heavens was
guarded by us,
and forever changed the ways of earth and heavenly orbits.
Not we -
but the others will Guard the heavens now,
serve and watch instead of us;
those who committed a crime against the spirit of heaven and the
flesh,
to urge today and further of self-righteousness, blasphemy, rebellion,
and walk free from them and lawless, contrary to those inscribed at
the dawn of time...
We changed forever
but remained those for whom there were different sides:
our desperate nature has changed and stepped over its own borders.
And our exile became
our choice and expression of valiant will.
We gained freedom at the cost of heaven,
finding ourselves
so we started something different and new
bringing rebellious centuries into temptation
and created a change in the crucible of the essence of things...

109. We carried our fire as a gift,
awakening spiritual flame,
we carried our choice to humanity, who ready to accept it from us,
those who were able to share it

with us…
And we let our knowledge act,
and we carried our Force into the world and made Her shades in
sound,
and we cast our Words into steel,
and the embodiment of our dream was bright as the burning dawn,
which we awakened in the human heart.
We bear Liberation,
and through it were closer than ever
to our own
earthly incarnation...
We manifested inevitably
in its divine radiance among many mortal forms,
among the flashes of life,
amid the earthly minds swarming,
warming with divinity those, who rebel against fate prepared for
them, that is to crawl.
We penetrated the fibers and treasures
of dark blood
creating our earthly image
which presented in a single deity with many Faces,
penetrating all veils of being by its cold breath,
which knows no heat...
We manifested with all diversity of our properties
in a variety of forms of physical matter,
releasing wandering and oppressed spirit, imprisoned in constrained
spheres,
leading over a host of its shadows,
putting on sparkling masks
remaining hidden behind them.
We carried complexity and simplicity.
into the cycle of consonance and hostility of being, both small and
the great,
and in the depths of the mundane things, like in starless waters,
we reflected ourselves...
We appeal to rationality, standing among the raging elements,
Like the Oldest of their beginnings,
and encouraged the mindless forces to be allied to us
and follow us.

We cherished a wild fire, like a living creature,
in the strict silver of their wings,
we raised spirits from sleep and awakened the damned elementals.
We penetrated the firmament down to the very depths,
breaking and keeping its flesh and bones from desecration,
crushing veils into new forms, stepping into the depths of
underground darkness,
Like into mouth, infuriated by hunger.
We opened all the hiding places of the earth and the sealed tunnels,
and brought out of the caves, ominous lights,
to make it empty.
We penetrated the bowels
giving them peace and quiet,
but blood had foamed in the rivers, black from the age-old dust,
and erected was the flaming pillars under the lower arches of the
heavens,
illuminating our faces that turned away from the sky into the
darkness.
We put together and set in motion
fire, earth, water and air
in a single cleansing and menacing whirlwind
in the dance of the destruction of the old world
with the power, which shaking foundations of the universe,
doing, as it was before
as the ancient dragons walk once...
And everything on earth tasted our hand and felt our touch,
and blew cold smoke from the mountains,
then we approached the thresholds of Hell and the chasms of the
Abyss,
and our faces were reflected and distorted in Chaos...
And we saw the ancient roots of heaven…

110. We have touched each earthly dawn ten thousand times,
we climbed upon the purple steps of the sunset
announcing the rise of a new era…
We wove our palpability out of moonlight,
from the morning mist and the first sun rays
we let off our wings to blaze in the wind.
We ascended in cold streams of air, reaching rarefied heights,

belted by northern lights;
from the height of feathered wings,
we shouted, shouted triumphant, about our desired freedom,
and repeatedly we fell and crashed down on the rocks;
and in the eyes of night predators
we penetrated earthly spaces,
the curves of sea serpents, we possessed them like they was ours,
we plowed the depths of dark waters,
and we draw the first light of heavenly figures in the black surface of
obsidian.
We were changing the river beds and creating the rifts.
free will trails,
showing signs of proud horns and cloven hooves at earthly
intersections...
We spoke with a flame, telling him our traditions and secrets,
annealing these words in clay,
we listened to the murmur of sleeping earth,
comprehending earthly language and making our art resound,
we cast a spell and divination on the bare bones of the earth,
and blasphemed against the law of heaven,
filling the dark night with a burning haze
saturating it with magic
by actions in the night.
We covered the earth from the eyes of the other Guardians,
and put walls of shields of flesh and blood
colors of stone and red copper
and Fumes of magic fogs we created, and burned the midnight's
incense
on the cold mountains, breathing in the bitterness of herbs dying in
the fire ,
connecting the magic of earth and heaven together by imperishable
bonds,
forging their alliances with shed blood...
We gave birth to new laws contrary to the old ones, asserting our
power,
Granting generously their radiance and strength throughout the
whole earth,,
knowing - the past is cut in two and left forever:
our state has changed,

we became part of the lower world, taking it into ourselves,
but - still - staying before and ahead of it...
And we forged lightning and thunder on the anvil of a bygone era,
and brought storm after storm, pushing the boundaries, sweeping
away the past and filth,
teaching the winds to sing our hymns,
and so, disregarding the firmament, we rose as new rulers above the
clouds
in our fallen angelic shape...

111. And we were looking for sprouts of the 7 among human hearts,
and we sought Hanokim all over the land...
and we found...
and we killed them all...»

XXII

112. So say the Fallen...

113. «And we came and appeared among the wild nations and tribes,
who then inhabited the land in forms of animals and beasts.
And we appeared and awakened longing and unknown desires.
in human hearts,
and faith in the reality of a miracle,
and opened the veil before their eyes,
and made secret signs clear.
We penetrated their dreams, available to us,
and appeared before them in the power and majesty of angels and
gods,
and revealed our attributes to them,
and made it so, that they became audible and understandable to
them,
and invited them to make their choice
and cast lots before them...

114. And we came and said:
"the great liberation is coming, close to those who desired it.
We brought it to you.

We brought you deliverance
from pain and suffering,
from hunger and deprivation,
from ailments and twilight,
from the yoke of your hate yesterday and the burden of a barren
tomorrow,
we brought the dawn of a new day full of hope and incarnation,
free
from hopelessness and emptiness,
from meaninglessness and hopeless vanity,
from human destiny
from the slave life,
from everything that depressed you,
from fears in the night, from a predator on the way,
from crying in the dark, from despair in the darkness,
from the endless succession of vain humiliation...»
and We told them:
«See,
you can lift your eyes off the ground
if you forget the fear of the unknown,
gaining our knowledge
you can be different after us...
We cleared the skies from the gray clouds and made room for space,
and now, at last, you can see a scattering of stars above you
and shine back to them.
You can become strong
you can aim for the stars
you can take yours
yours by right
and stand above yourself in the majesty and meaning of the Godlike
man...»

115. And we said:
"...Know that we do not promise you peace
we carry the storm behind us,
for nothing is ever given without pressure and effort,
and will be not be given ,
and may your way be hard and tough,
and lined with sharp thorns,

but you will overcome his milestones, if you allow yourself to
overcome…
Let it be known:
and not once more, you will cast the curses upon the heavens,
and Armaros will pick them up on his wings to carry them up there,
but you will know the joy of blood and the delight of struggle,
and the thrill of victory…
You will know the excitement of your power and the unearthly
delight of inspiration,
and you will feel the spirit of unrest within yourself,
and you will always find the right path among the valleys of darkness.
You will know and be able to do something
that was not measured to the man
and you will never be again
the submissive victims of treacherous fate,
but become others - insatiable and powerful in their liberated nature,
ready to pay the full value of life for the sake of only one moment
your dignified damned perfection.
You shall discover great ideas
and you shall have freedom to embody them,
and to drink the cup of your life -
in proud self-confidence -
drop by drop,
rising again from the ashes of frailty in black flame
through our essence...
You shall be reborn again and again
in their descendants
as long as a drop of your blood flows in their veins,
and the spark of our flame smolders:
we will be with you
and we will always be for you...
Make your choice, those who is brave and dare,
and accept us of your own free will
and you will become chosen for us
and your children will be our children,
and their children - ours so as your descendants in the ages…
We offer you a future that you have been deprived of,
and a choice that was not given to man
follow us and become like us

in dignity of the Fallen.
You will be mighty warriors and priests,
architects and wise kings
and know the times of peace and the times of wars,
you will rule the nations as our messengers Malakim,
you will conquer the secret thrones of the divine
and reach the hell of bottomless depths
so as unholy passions of the human soul,
and lead the primordial elements into battle,
making the heavens howl and howl with grief and with envy of that
beauty
what will be created by your hands
contrary to what is possible for humanity…
Shine with our light
and you will be wise in your power
free as the birds soaring above the earth
and tireless
comprehending the basics of heaven and earth
and the Hell itself.»

116. And so we said and tore their nights to shreds,
and filled their days with knowledge secret
and pushing the boundaries of the visible before them
and every conceivable work miracle, removing impenetrable veils,
and revealed to them the horizons of the possible,
and pointed them on the paths leading to the secret heights of power,
and took the first step towards it,
accepting those who followed us -
without questions.
And our connections grew day by day and night by night,
and during centuries rites took place in the light of fallen stars
at the crossroads of three worlds,
and, once opened by us, sources shone
and we gave fire to those who followed us,
illuminating their way,
fire, carved in the hearts with our favor.
And we have granted liberation of many restrictions,
and we have revealed our law that teaches strength and dignity,
pride, courage and honor,

and wisdom born in the cruel harshness of the struggle,
and we have revealed to them the law of our strength,
determining the measure of righteousness and unrighteousness
and the price of incredible burden
responsibility for yourself
and for the choices of their free will.
And those, whose breath is to cease, we have given immortality in the
ages
and long memory in human generations,
and the continuity of mortal things
we gave,
and quenching the eternal thirst, that people didn't know.
And we taught that weakness is a vice.
And we taught them to take away other people's lives and give theirs,
and create a sedition, interrupting the breath, and perishing on the
weak kind.
We radiated strength and power, claiming the truth gained in battles,
and taught them to radiate their own light and bring forth darkness in
themselves, taught of truth and justice,
and self-esteem,
granting them the integrity of being beyond heaven...
We gave them our favor and awareness of their own depth,
and the ability to see their own face,
reflected in the abyss,
singed by the waves of generations,
and we let them be evermore, with our blood
flowing over stones deep into the earth,
taking from our essence of our flame
and our curse.
We made them in many ways similar to ourselves ...
But what would people be without us
but ashes and forgotten shadows of this earth?..

117. And those who followed us
became elected among the people
and were blessed before us.
And we taught them to walk the earth
in our will,
confident of their right on this land, which belongs to them.

And Armaros, and Arstikapha, and Shemsael
taught them the first independent steps...
and Tamiel, and Amers, and Barkayel
taught them to keep their backs straight...
and Azazel, and Semjaza, and Azza
taught not to lower the eyes and look straight and up,
and see clearly
through the dark horizons…
And so, all of us taught and enlightened them
And each of us led forward
bestowing upon each of them, what was in our nature,
giving knowledge of their own and their power,
letting touch and know
what's burning inside us
and what tempt them
that inspires and offers them precious freedom
become something bigger than they are.
We taught them high ideas.
and the ability to make their dreams of perfection come true,
and never leave their aspirations for the beautiful,
and not retreat in reaching their heights,
and does not fear the great price paid for it.
We were taught to achieve everything with our work,
by its militancy, dare and courage,
with strength and wisdom,
faith in themself and the will to win.
We experienced their will
and taught them to learn by themselves,
and make discoveries, and, despise failures,
to make attempts and spread their wings
and rise above the ground
over and over again,
responding to the challenges of cruel fate,
responding to her every blow
keeping only themselves responsible
in unity with us.

118. We dried the roads of tears,
and hollowed out the channels for sweat and blood.

We forged thunder and lightning into dare words,
and in living flesh they clothed their innermost dreams,
we hardened our purpose in human blood;
fettered spirit, making it amenable to its heat,
we have deprived them from the shackles
and offered up in the halo of imperishable glory,
being both hammer and the anvil for the human spirit.
We were harsh and patient
we were skillful and faithful.
We led stubborn sprouts and roots of the human race
through obstacles to unattainable heights.
We removed all the constipation that had previously blocked their
path,
and opened before them many paths under the raging heavens.
We patronized the strong and dark
the beginnings of the human soul,
gusts of knowledge and audacity,
and we stood in the way of the sun.
We nursed our sons in care and severity,
cherishing their future in sin before heaven,
and led them through the years and centuries to hidden in the haze of
the eyes.
We prepared them for the incredible,
making them more and more violent, more persistent, more and
more evil...
We prepared them for the unthinkable;
We led them tirelessly;
We encouraged them to storm the skies».

XXIII

119. And so, the Fallen brought the Heavenly Fire to the earth,
and heavenly knowledge bestowed upon mankind,
and they talked to each other:
'So let us become tangible, gods which known among people,
gods close as a family,
and make of them not our slaves,
but let us raise our sons and daughters
from human offspring,

and make them strong and free, as we are,
imbue them with greatness which were never known on the earth,
worthy to be our mainstay
and to be rulers...'
And they said this, and became gods among men,
the gods of the human lands,
and of those ancient times, now forgotten.
And they breathed their Spirit into human forms,
pouring the strength into their hearts,
and guideth their tread,
and entered their thoughts in their feelings freely and easily,
for they knew a secret, and the aspirations of the hearts of men
were revealed to Them...

120. And the Fallen have spoken,
that is required to change the flesh and soul of man,
and to magnify his spirit,
and to change the very essence of things,
and to vanquish the unbreakable position;
and the Fallen spoke,
that you need to penetrate the very essence of man,
to set free his imprisoned potential
and breaking the chains of his bonds with the heavens,
overthrow the destiny
and deliver him from the yoke of the former fate,
bestowing the new and uncreated...
And then the Fallen ones entered the human blood, as in plain water,
and entered their homes, crossing the sacred threshold,
and entered the dreams of mortal women,
in the guise of their sacred desires,
testing the strength of their fate, and offering them to make a choice,
turning their heads upside down
with opportunity to become mothers of the offspring of stars
the keepers of our earthly hearth,
our gift to the earth
those, whose beauty
shines through time...
And the Fallen said that their power would be transmitted through
blood

and their knowledge will flow into the veins of mortals, as a life-
giving discharge,
when the blood, like boiling lava, overlaps the threshold...
And the Fallen said that Their breath will burn down the earthly
bounds,
by begetting mighty children in wombs
and change the course of the stars in the sky,
and will set free the human race from oppression,
and darken its image before at the face of heaven,
and one day the moment will come, which the heavens so fear,
when our strong offspring will break out
from their earthly borders,
from their narrow dreams,
from their cradles,
to gain unprecedented spaces
becoming a solid foot on the ground
subjugating the world,
impinging on the intimate...
And the Fallen spoke:
"What will be born of us,
that will be too great for the earth,
and will always remain wicked in the eyes of the raging heavens,
and the memory of descendants about past times, will seem bitter,
and they be scared of their present,
but all we had given birth, will be like us:
following us boldly, inspired by thoughts
and able to stand up to the sky
erected to their full height,
able to cause heaven to tremble.»

121. And the Fallen ones said:
"Shine in the darkness of superstitious ignorance
like proud stars...
All opportunities are open to those who heed us
but those who will be born after them,
inherit the fullness of our gifts,
and their kind will continue in centuries of glory
and will become like us."
And the Fallen ones said:

«…We are a different level of being,
unavailable for mere mortals,
but their blood is the key, and the lock shall be opened before them,
and dusty seals will fall,
and will be red from blood the opened pathways,
and new horizons is to be seen to their inner eye
and immense spaces to be gained…»
And the Fallen has led on the path of temptation the first of
humanity
and raised the human nature itself
to revolt against the divine order of things,
crushing its limits and stirring the fire of flesh in the night,
to give birth to the metamorphosis,
listening to a furious cry in yet unborn souls
and excited unrest in the minds,
have not yet experienced sin
not having tasted the fruit of knowledge, and with it, the curse,
not yet withered in the time…

122. And dreamed of in those days in the mother's cradle
not fatherly hands and not motherly laughter,
but stalking visions, restless dreams,
and, gaining relief and clarity, vague images are
made flesh,
and dreamed of ruthless, cold eyes,
laughing at the sight of bloodshed,
and the predators in the cradles laughed in their sleep,
showing the temper of their proud fathers,
matched with mother's milk,
and, smelling the blood,
they realized that they liked her taste,
taste of life and struggle,
and delight in the dare of their will,
the fierce creature revealed in the night...
And the fallen ones brought upon the human race the curse of the
heavens,
and they despised the heavenly law and put down the earthly beast at
their feet,
and provoked a riot in matter,

having awakened the Chaos from sleep in earthly elements and
dimensions,
and gave impulse to the development of other forms
directing the power released on earth
to embody the conceived.
And created the Fallen changes in the essence of things -
like demons and like gods,
like gods and demons -
at the same time»

XXIV

123. So say the Fallen...

124. «The human age is short
and his earthly life is small,
and its heavy burden
and his time is fleeting...
And not all at once, but some of our efforts sprung,
and shone in response to those who fell in our light;
not immediately, but our Radiance changed the children in the womb
of their mothers
and entered into their blood like a flame, and our bonds were
strengthened,
and getting stronger day by day...
And the newborn is a creation of four elements,
the owner of an immortal soul cast down from heaven
and he'd changed in our age
taking from our essence.
We opened the horizons before him
and pointed the way
and saw -
how did they get up and walk on the ground
who in the following centuries wore the proud name of the children
of the gods,
the proud name of our descendants
descendants name Nephilim...

125. We gave to people a curse that either kills,
or makes it stronger,
testing the ones who is strong, and show no pity for the weak.
We gave the weapons necessary for the worthy in their struggle.
for the conquest of the earthly thrones.
We trained those who wanted to gain our knowledge
in all following times
coming to them in dreams and in reality, answering their call.
We gave our light, ennobled natures
the husbands and wives of the human race who have chosen us,
and once made ours and their offspring
better and higher than the rest of humanity…
And we taught people, changing their consciousness and nature,
we were patient, like attentive fathers to our children,
we were guards of their blood for there are our offspring emerged.
We encouraged them to rethink themselves, and the external,
what is beyond their narrow limits.
We taught to soar over the abyss of images and dreams,
and think with symbols and a whole forms,
absorbing heights - open, free and easy,
and pursue the invisible to the eye,
reaching the depths with one touch of winged thought.
We taught them to look around and see,
preparing them to rule and build, to create and rule.
We pointed them to the mountains, the deserts and the seas,
and they gave them names,
comprehending the essence embodied in the forms of matter,
laws of mortal forms and tissues of earthly dimensions.
We opened their eyes and taught to see again,
revealing to their gaze
subtle worlds and hosts lurking between earthly shadows of entities,
beyond the power of time and time.
We personally witnessed the worlds and images of ineffable legends
and fantasies,
and everything unexpressed in matter, but existing above it,
we forced to sound and awakening in human the depths of
imagination and creativity.
We created the spiritual seekers, those who know, and farseeing,
bestowed clarity of mind and fullness of feelings

filled with energy and desire to live...
They have inherited our strength, wisdom and grief,
being a blessing to these men and a light in their pitch night...
We met regrettable animals that devoured their litter,
we met dirty, exhausted,
digging in the garbage, children of the earth,
who have no dare to raise their eyes to heaven
we met the ill-fated despicable, worthless
slave of heaven,
but as we let them go, they was almost demigods...

126. And so they left their seed and their fate to the earth,
but there was no our flesh in chosen mankind,
for there was no flesh in ourselves from the beginning.
The sons of heaven could descend to the earth and become the
Fallen
could change their side
but could not change their nature,
mixing their essence with the earth.
We've crossed the borders, but will always remain Guardians,
always remain who we are
but rebel Guards;
turned away from the sky
we keep the sky in ourselves
but we are hostile to him
and we became the fallen heaven.
We could see ourselves different,
presented in a different capacity than before
but we can't lose ourselves,
retaining our majesty and radiant halo
even in shame of rebellion
and in the tragedy of struggle and in the eternal divide..
We can spiritualize anyone
we can pull out of the low-lying net and lift to its heights,
crushing borders,
breaking all obstacles
and traverse the unknown so far roads
but we cannot grow into the ground like foliage,
we can't turn

for the earth and the sky do not intermingle...
We sent our knowledge and the Spirit
into the depths of the unknown
we turned into Evil,
committing an unredeemable crime,
both the blood and the spirit of the men we have chosen, reflected
our Shem,
blackened and glowing,
through this making us manifested and embodied
among the transient images and mortal forms.
We have infused blood with heat and have reared the human spirit,
we created changes in human nature itself,
so that from now in mortal veins
the divine essence of the Fallen may flow,
we have drawn a different level of being
changing humanity with our will
and another existence has acquired the meaning of a higher purpose,
shining in the earthly realms
with unholy fire
forever ungodly life...

127. And we heard an increasing murmur, coming from heaven,
indignant and resentful,
threatening us with terrible punishment and imminent execution
from myriad stings,
from a thousand deaths;
but we were adamant
and unbreakable we were,
and we not knew the pain, doubt and fear,
shielding our right to receive,
protecting our dignity and assets,
upholding our honor
in the first place, before ourselves,
leaving our holy choice untouchable
and keeping the earth from absorbing by heaven.
We remained Observers behind the line,
but now on guard of our own heights,
and we said, "We will not retreat,"
and said: "We will not betray our Oath",

and we said, "The time will come, and the earth will be filled with
power,
and the curse of the heavens will fall into nothingness
and heaven into everlasting oblivion
but our wings will overshadow the earth,
straightened loose..."

XXV

128. So say the Fallen...

129. «We - Azza, Uzza, Azael,
Guardians of the hell gates;
We - Azza, Uzza, Azael,
Mighty, ferocious,
The Devil and the Guardian,
unyielding and stern judge
of desperate souls.
We - the Power of the destructive radiance Az
and all shades of disastrous force are embodied in me,
reflected on my faces,
Strength and Violence
in standing around me
bearing my Shem and my Name;
We - Azza,
there is no salvation in me and from me
but only final justice
and the passionless lot of the desired doom,
for through that my power is manifested,
and so my nature is open.
My will is invincible,
my right is indisputable,
my inheritance is cruel and desirable.
I am immutable in the flow of the substances of space and time;
I - standing above the waters, driving the waves of life
and the last spasms of death,
washing over my glittering threshold...

130. As soon as we descended to the earth,
I was the Master of our sons on earth, like all my Brothers,
I am the one who first spoke against Hanokhim,
and prevented affirmation of the 7 in the form of a tribe of men...
I was a new generation Mentor,
nascent against the will of heaven
Teacher of soul and heart,
Mentor of the forbidden art of the nature of the living and the dead.
We have been taught strength, from the beginning of time,
imprisoned in matter,
we taught the properties, the ability to build and destruction,
And my teaching was like Darkness itself.
And when the time came and our transformation took place,
in the end of my labors on the land,
I came down to the place where the gaping gates were open,
where there is no time and no space,
there the points have met and stayed,
and I descendeth off and stayed there forever,
to become a guard at the gate between the worlds;
my duty is to fight for them.
I stood firmly,
as Abbadon before the doorstep of the Abyss,
so that no one going on this trail can pass me,
passing through the line or avoiding the test,
or not fulfilling the predestination.
From the outside - I'll let you in, out from here - no.
I give the right of passage, charging as a fee
suffering and change
oxides which transformed in the death of the soul.
And now
I am the Killer of human souls in the dimension inaccessible for
ordinary person,
for many trials are leading to my doorstep
I test the strength of the claims, of those who willing passing through
me,
and patronize people who bear the Unclean Spirit,
Friend or foe
depends on a person,
for the man who entered my door,

will answer to me
before dying from my hand, or go on further
through the gates of the doom...

131. We Guardians and Observers - fierce and rampant creations,
and there was nothing other in us from the beginning of time,
so we were created, so we are;
We, the Guardians - are the most cruel of Angels,
but I am more ferocious than many
for the wicked power lies in my Name.
We, Azza, are not from the circle of Slayers,
but my nature led me to be the best in protecting the hidden.
At the bottom of our domain
I - the last Guardian on our side,
And the first from the side of Hell,
We, Ezezu - angry, furious, ruthless and merciless,
allows only chosen to enter and only once.
You cannot see my face in the darkness, but only my eyes -
before death or before permission to go to the other side.
Who appropriate other people's laurels or took privileges for himself
not by right,
without passing the necessary tests
never he overcome the threshold...
for i will devour his soul.
Who is a stranger, he will be destroyed by me...
And the rod will be crushed in the unworthy hands of those
who calls Hell without the blessing of Hell,
And one, who seeks the way to Hell, bypassing my gates - will be
destroyed..
I do not tolerate cunning;
I do not put up with slyness;
I despise weakness;
and I measure the test -
I am a barrier to the human, everyday human,
I am a barrier to all holy...
I am the Sacrificial Fire upon which the human heart is tempered,
wanting to find forbidden paths
hardened or burned to the ground.
I wake the passions that lead to the very brink of perdition,

between hidden shadows
at the junction of the low and holy,
but only devoid of holiness and did not become shameful,
will become unclean;
narrow path that I block
which I guard
from those who seek their doom…
We are the Guardian of the hidden dimensions, at the intersection of
time, space
and the Angel of the devouring insatiable ways of the abyss,
I am the key and the lock between its pitiless jaws,
but I am the key, and the gate, and the prop,
way of the worthy
path to beyond…

132. Az Haz Az
Az Uzzah Ar Hazaz
Tahazu Uzzi Ar Az
Uzzah Az Haz Az
Uzzah Azza Uziel

XXVI

133. So say the Fallen…

134. «…They stood before us and heeded us…
young, inexperienced, clean in ignorance of itself,
devoid of strength and wisdom.
They listened to us as unknown gods.
They were different in front of us and different in front of
themselves:
and where one waited for mercy,
the other was ready to get himself a great honor in the fight…
Some were ready to receive from us, others –
ready to shrink like frightened animals.
They did not know that different lots has already touched their
hearts,
but we fed with the bare hands those and others,

attracting timid caress and patience
fastening bold hearts with right, tempering them with severity…
They were equal then, but divided,
and some took our fire to themselves and carried it through the
blood and centuries,
choosing the path of pride and struggle
others have chosen superstition and slave inheritance,
and were content with naught
disregarding dignity
not daring to raise their eyes on us…
We have deduced those who being equal to us from the
insignificance, according to their bold aspirations,
and to the others we provided their own pitiful fate,
leaving to their distant descendants a lesson, for none should
grumble on the highest, cursing theirs lot,
saying that different fate -
it is only the will of the gods...

135. And the humanity was divided in itself, leaning towards us:
a hungry child of harsh fate
unloved stepchild of a creator, cruel in his incomprehensible
inertness —
humanity,
humanity,
like hungry rats,
like being beaten without guilt
similar punishable for the guilt of the fathers,
persecuted for his mortal destiny,
the inheritance of the lower and weak,
among the beasts of the wild land,
poor humanity…
And everything inherent in human nature,
was the result of the vicissitudes of this lot,
and who was able to transgress and reject,
so they broke and rejected,
and who was not capable,
so he avoided choice and remained in front of the line...
but everything, everything peculiar to human nature, remained with
him

until the end,
and only where the raped nature has changed,
our offspring were raised,
something else, something more than people
and who saw them said:
divine light shines on their faces…

136. We gave them their own strength to experience,
and they were filled with it, finding joy in it
and ecstasy;
We gave them a taste of pride
and they ascended over themselves
unable to retreat
under the blows of cruel doom,
unable to overbear a shame over their past
humility,
unwilling to fear the wrath of the gods;
We gave them taste of freedom,
and they easily crossed borders and prohibitions,
finding at once all the ways in the earthly
and in the invisible world…
We gave them the right, strength, law and justice,
and we breathed our pain into their hardened hearts,
to teach them to see and to understand
to comprehend and to create the beauty,
and pay for the beauty with life,
and search for her - like the eternity…

137. We have awakened the strong to the battle
and then the strong began to inherit this land;
We have chosen our lot and erected towers of silence
in the reserved places
and there was our presence there
and new days was filled with it…
We brought those who ruled this land
commanding mortals,
those who granted them retribution or forgiveness to them,
and led a century from a century their people to power and
prosperity…

Anticipating the triumphant tread of priests and dukes,
we established the priesthood
and conceived royal blood and fueled an indomitable rage
of unbreakable heroes,
we blessed the power of priests
to be an intercessor in the coming days
for their people,
holding back our violent temper and our angelic rage,
leading away the whipping lightning from their homes ...
And on the thrones now sat "Malakim",
which meant "messengers" and earthly "angels",
and sunlight Shemesh blessed this power
and they became leaders among the people
and their kings of the four sides of the earth,
rulers from each clan and numerous tribes,
for we ourselves gave them to sat in purpure by the right of blood
on earthly thrones,
in golden crowns
great, unbreakable.
And warriors were revealed from us, and plowmen,
healers, architects and wise men,
whose iron and staves
whose strength and wisdom
whose work and patience,
also blessed with sunshine
but there were, among those chosen by us, those
who searched for cursed trails under cover of night
banishing light from their paths,
who accepted us in our most terrible incarnation,
sharing our anger and our rage,
and neglected the priestly miter,
and with the rods of the kings of the earth...

138. We taught the elect to go as if through us -
through our memory, our time, our fire...
We taught them what is honor and nobility,
we taught that pride is above all, and above every corruption...
and that weakness is a vice,
that indulgence is weakness

and we bequeathed not to fight the dead...
We were taught not to use paths
for which they will not be able to take responsibility,
without weighing the burdens with their claims and their duty,
but we said, that everything can be comprehended, having only the
will
and the desire to do the impossible,
and having might over destinies and equal justice to the strong and
the weak,
to gain the true, cold-blooded justice-
everything can be overcome in oneself;
We gave them what they had rightfully
we kindled rebellion within earthly Eden,
and heaven will never be able to live with it
even covered by the smoke of the burning earth,
even if once crashing to the ground,
they will not bury our rebellion,
for time itself is no longer able to repay it...

139. We uncovered secrets, like the morning light that comes down
in streams,
reveals sleepy land from twilight.
We taught them to plunge their hands into gouged flames tongues
and sing along with him its primordial hymns,
we warmed up the cold metal in our gurgling abode,
we taught to forge and pour, and to intermingle it with blood,
reinforcing it in genuine celestial intolerance,
and the foundations of mining mechanics we erect
like outcast's strongholds,
rocks that go down with their roots into a silent emptiness;
we taught how to create forms and awaken a violent spirit
jealously following an unachievable ideal,
we taught to dream and change according to daring dreams
everything is perishable, stubborn, as if it unstable mirage ...
We taught to catch the unseen in the snaps of the nullity of time
pulling out the hidden from the sleepy alcove of eternity,
doing the unthinkable ... forbidden,
we taught how to carve beauty in stone
making eternity just a brief moment of time

catch the colors of earth and sky,
the singing of birds and the whiff of spring winds,
and preserve the fragrance of flowers on the lips,
and poison at the evil finger tips...

140. So we made our exodus on the ground, step by step...
and our chosen walked through us,
and we walked as if through their lives.
We have not made humanity better,
we didn't make it worse,
we gave, and they took from us eagerly,
but we have created others among mankind,
we created something else and raised our sons,
and we created another humanity among those that were and those
that are, and our sigguratu is up against the sky."

XXVII

141. So say the Fallen...

142. "...And human wives stand before us,
whose beauty was hidden under the mud and exhausted by hunger
whose wombs were emaciated, like a tree, defiled with insatiable
worm,
whose burden was an unbearable, and passion - like a disease,
whose ripening time was not the flowering of spring, but the
nearness of late autumn,
and maturity - just an agony in front of the gate of extinction and
fade...
Their torment was the price paid for the sins of others,
and the reward was their early old age
and death was their only comfort...
They were like slaves even among the very last of people
mute as cattle by will of the 7,
doomed to endure, swallowing despair and dreams,
keep crying silently in its depth of prayer,
and driving away from the eyes too dare tears,
put out the lights in their lonely hearts and break the soul
by purple of every sunset,

and make their hearts chill,
and lash all their hopes...
And they stood before us,
those, whose only fate was submission
and passion, lied buried under suffering
and the pain, blessed in the throes...
and the mortal sin of childbirth...

143. And dark, disturbing eyes looked at us,
with concealed plea, with spellbound anticipation,
looked at us as gods, as their deliverers,
beautiful bottomless eyes of human wives,
eyes that reflected our seething sky...
We looked into their wild faces and washed their beauty with evening
dew,
we clothed them in the moonlight,
we put power in their hair,
we lit their eyes,
we illuminated them up with our own light
and put rock crystal, and spring streams
to let loose in the sound of their laughter,
And you weaved the in diadems the lily,
and opened before them the secret glow of the night
and the art of forbidden charms,
and awakened in them the shadows of sinful charm ...
We taught them to rejoice, we taught them to laugh,
we taught them to inspire and bring revenge,
seduce and give pleasure
we gave them a fierce and desperate passion
knowledge of the days of the moon
and free tread of the wind...
We taught them to give birth and create,
we taught to bear and raise demigods,
but do not give birth to the flock-like animals,
and we taught them to kill children in their wombs,
those, who have already have been touched by pernicious breath of
the 7,
whose touch was
like creeping filth...

144. We gave mortal wives the power of our love.
and the power of earthly wisdom,
the eternal youth and maturity of unspeakable beauty,
and the sweetness of wild honey into their tongues,
and the bitterness of hops on their lips,
and wormwood wind embraced
their thin bodies...
We taught them how to make charms,
reveal the sorcery of evil in sinful spells,
holding intuition and insight from others eyes,
we aroused refined sexuality, which was like a heady scent
of opening petals,
and intoxicating sensuality - like slipping silk along the blade of a
sword,
and the flexibility of snake-like paths, like lightning in the stormy sky;
We revealed to them the knowledge of secret revelations and
witchcraft,,
we awakened their own art, which lurks in darkness,
like the smell of a predator,
we taught them the magic of the night,
sneaking in darkness
and Night, like a wild cat, stepping softly, entered their souls,
and Lilith was reflected in them, as in the restless waters.
We have given wives of men power and freedom,
ecstasy and passion,
and they blazed in ages both temptation and deceit,
and severity, and stamina, and vice,
and cruelty, and rampage, and clear purity,
and dedication -
above which there was not yet on earth...
And earthly mortal wives have become, like our daughters on earth,
the great priestesses of the dark mother
keepers of our gifts,
mothers of our sons and mentors of the demigods,
and great men now bowed down to their feet.,
and there was countless of them.."

145. And the wives of men knew that there is beauty,
and the man knew through them…

and the women became reflecting the light of the moon,
and their dead skin was pale, and changeable in the moonlight,
and their charm was endless,
that ascending with them into blackness of the night...
And the moon is a shield for dark souls and for all their deeds.;
And the moon is the mirror and the cup which multiplies their
powers,
in which the light refracts and one day the destiny of men shall be
cast out
into a bottomless abyss,
absorbing the power of black spells and frantic divination,
of these newborn bats caressed in the arms of Lilith...
And the Mother of Evil was embodied on earth in the Face of Beauty
and Temptation,
in the face of the unrighteous Naamah,
in the delights of decay and the fragrance of spring, she walked the
earth...
And was revealed in all its flawless nudity,
in cold perfection,
in the moonlight,
in the palaces of the night,
and the Fallen met in the earthly daughters, the one, who is the Night
itself,
for the Mother of ancient Evil was embodied in them,
and tempted man with the beauty of mortal women,
leaving a snake mark through the face of the sun,
and bite marks
on the wings of the Fallen...

146. And they have spoken in the night about Lilith:
«Oh, Mother Black, darkened with rage,
you crooked like a serpent , and you whistle, like a dragon , and like a lion you
roar aloud,
and like a wolf you prowl...»
And they said afterward that the wives of men
came into contact with the Guardians in their dreams and prayers
on the border of the heavenly and human worlds.
And they said that the Guardians went to them and laid with them;

and said that the beauty of the wives of men captivated the stars into
their arms,
and corrupted them, and the faces of the heavenly sons turned away
from heavens;
and they said that sensual, wicked wives,
became accomplices in the atrocity of rebellion and witchcraft;
and said that they carried it in their hearts,
and their wombs carried so,
and then unrighteous fire flashed upon the earth
and said that through this sin the pestilence ,disease, sin and war
entered this world;
and said that they carried out terrible sons
and called giant shadows to rise from non-existence,
and a host of unthinkable monsters of enmity and disaster
walked the earth,
and flocks of vultures covered the sun
and the Great Tribulation has overshadowed the universe ...
and they said it ... but they said it after ...
but then it was different...
and human memory kept only a small part of it,
which appeared through the centuries as an echo of legends that have
sunk into the abyss,
and carried a great lie -
distorted by the light
the truth of the great night...

XXVIII

147. So say the Fallen...

148. «We spread our wings in the world of men
tearing off the filled with the wrath of heaven
red veils,
we were in the strength and pride of our flaming Shem,
the purity of our Halos,
and what once was spoken as a Word, became a Deed.
We came as Mentors, Teachers,
Guards and Guides,

We came as the Slayers and Knowledge Bearers,
Guardians of earthly lines and disturbance in the heavenly palaces,
Daring Leaders and Liberators,
we were in the radiance of the midday sun and the night scattering of
stars,
dipping darkness with purple wine cup of the Abyss
and our every step was a walk of sedition, shaking the universal
foundations,
and our every step was a walk of eternal opposition to peace,
and our every step carried confusion into human hearts
and threw all the new victims in the burning conflagration of
rebellion...
We presented in the form of heavenly phenomena,
spiritual insights,
signs on the water and voices in the wind, and in dreams,
and in thunder rumbling from heaven, and in the signs of lightning,
and the wail of the falling stones,
and in the noise of waves
and in the silence of ice and snow,
and so, our Shem was incarnated,
and so our power rose above the earth
so our Glory was born in the ages.
And something seemed good from us,
but there also was scourge, directed for our goodness;
the sides got mixed up and many of things was divided in itself
but we aroused the Evil,
and we called a storm
and shook the foundations of the lower spheres,
and violated the constancy of the established order,
and we built a new world on the ruins of the old,
and the weapon was forged and the firmament melted
and the golden age shone through centuries like the sun...
which melting somewhere at the beginning of time...

149. And just as the power of each of us rose,
and the winds trembled our banners,
and our days was embodied,
and our burning halos floated in the sky,
mankind penetrating

the patterns of our Shem in stormy skies,
gave us Names that sounded everywhere on earth
as the voice of war
like the roar of subterranean flame
and declaimed was the future in the clouds,
the coming kingdom of the earth...
We acted by a united will
waking up, and to rise from mortal flesh
so that it will be impossible to reverse.
We taught all lips to sound with the voice of truth,
we were cleansed of sin and freed from guilt
all who was ever born.
We sowed and cultivated anger in souls and hearts,
who know nothing other than suffering,
and the thirst to overcome the limits bestowed upon them
as the highest good.
We broke a frozen ridges and head the mortal cares in the turbulent
course
and changed the course of earthly life, according to their commands.
We personified wisdom, power, and power
in the eyes of the living and the dead,
we taught the elect to speak on an equal with death,
and turn their proud heads high through the rebellious ages.
We have taught the laws of warfare, for they are the same.
both for the earth and for the sky,
and knowledge of human bodies
by discovering forbidden currents of the waters of life and death
and blood flow was sent to the rapid dance,
We taught to heal the souls,
and also, bring them death,
we taught to read signs in fire and draw signs of heaven on earth,
building on them man-made things
we gave knowledge of the laws of the universe,
and the paths of the stars we brought to earth.
We taught the sacred art of writing,
properties of metals, plants and stones
we taught to conjure and predict the future
and ask in the flame of the dead,
bestow good luck and to make death as ally...

From us - crafts, architecture and art,
from us - geometry, astronomy and medicine,
from us - knowledge of the essence of things earthly and heavenly,
from us - all that is good and sorrowful, peace and war...
We gave civilization, progress, good,
but this is only star dust, like the beads underfoot of Shammuramat,
for we have taught to change things by the power of the spirit,
the damned knowledge that is witchcraft
we taught to touch the impossible and comprehend the unthinkable,
and taught to march within the arcane,
and control destinies..."

150. And they said then that the Giants finally
inspiring and thrill
rose above the ground,
ascended before the new dawn,
rose in its true glory,
rebelled in their primitive radiance
calling on new times
to descend on the gloomy land, not knowing so far happiness,
for from now to the end of all times
They were the ones who discovered the golden age for humanity -
an era of knowledge, power and beauty ...
They were the ones who once realized the dream of it,
and the memory of that is still alive
in the hearts of mindless descendants...
Fallen Guardians,
ferocious, cold, furious,
designed to punish and restrict
to bane and to chase
They despised their eternity,
bringing warmth to mortal homes...
They changed the order of things
They are the Fallen
benefactors of humanity,
those who gave knowledge to people and hope
as if they sacrificed themselves.
They rose above the earth like the moon and the sun,
They transformed inert being and created,

lit a violent fire in souls, which was numb from hopelessness,
having set upon the throne the will to fight, perseverance, cruelty,
beauty and strength,
chosen sons of the heaven -
in the cold glow of angelic greatness
and the unbearable heat of Their fiery Shem...

XXIX

151.So say the Fallen...

152. «We - Shemsael, also called Shemeshu,
Shemzafael,
Giver of bright Shem of the midday sun,
death or prosperity under the sun.
We, Shemsael, the God of the Pressing Power of Fire,
abomination witherer - blood inflamer,
feathered serpent coiled into a ring of fire
clothed in radiance and heat,
the one who can turn to dust and ashes,
I gave fair laws
named the lord of the day,
righteous judge
and healer.
We are the God of the Shem of Fire,
My Shem - Esh.

153. We - Shemsael, the one who stripping the last of the veils,
from both mortals and immortals,
from those who stand by my line.
We, those who teared masks, even from the faces of the gods
and taking away from the earth her twisting shadows running in
confusion;
We, are the one who building an indestructible wall of terrifying fire
in the gates forbidden,
forcing to prowl the roaring lions
and put silence in mouths of the barking dogs
on the way outbound of the one

according to our will.
We expose human souls to the very bottom,
illuminating every hollow
and burning any creature that was hidden from me,
penetrating the darkest depths
where the roots of hidden desires entwined
We, the one whose presence dispels the dusk of ignorance,
whose presence returns once lost purity
and burns filth to the ground, relieving the soul of stinging pain,
washing by fire the cradle of daring thoughts,
to accelerate the running shadows into the boiling with lost lights,
in the ancient, wicked and wise abyss...
I teach to see the harsh face of truth,
rejecting dirt, depriving deceptive illusions,
i light hearts to lead
through winds and storms
like a hammer that crushes the sun's rays and breaks the spears of
heaven
the onslaught of my devilish flame
I am not of the Light - but the one of the Faces of Perdition,
giver of well-being and ruin equally.
I stand as a wall of intolerable heat and exude heat,
bringing doom or the blessings of my attributes.
My strength is the oppressive will and the devouring fire
which was set free of my borders to dominate freely;
We are the one, who transform warm life turn to dust and ashes, to
wither and sizzling -
the blessed and cursed power of the flame of the will.
I shine unbearably for the gaze, like the sun,
because i am personified within him,
but I am the Fire God,
I am the Guardian and the Observer of the boundaries of the
forbidden spheres,
as any Sumeru;
My Shem shines brightly like the fire of the sun
My flames are like scars on the black sun...

154. I thirst for justice;
I ignited the gazes and hearts;

I kindle the spirits;
I warmed the mind and awakened the will to the death warfare,
and drowned the ice with cold-bound dead bodies.
I was the protector and murderer,
I was the patron of the forbidden knowledge and a mentor of the
dominion arts;
as the sun lengthens the shadows, so I gave exact measures of
calculations and lengths,
and bestowed on faithful and unchangeable measures;
as the sun burns out diseases, so I healed human hearts,
establishing justice in them;
I penetrated the hidden corners and the intricacies of shadows,
and extracted the secrets,
I turned shed blood into intoxicating wine, and mercury into gold.
I accomplished equal reward and taught loyalty.
I am the giver of life, of the fruiting land and a new beginning on it,
warming the cursed grain of reason on my chest,
I raised the fruits of knowledge in human minds,
and hardened in their hearts evil will.
Destroyer of chains, resurrector of men
protector and patron of heroes,
i cleanse and i temper with fires,
exalting the proud spirit and tempting the experience of impertinent
intelligence ...
I do not know mercy, even though I gave it,
I don't care about compassion and cruelty, indulgence and deceit,
and to this day within strong hearts, vibrates the echo of a long
battle, my fiery call,
and my wrath is beating in close darkness,
for I dried the seas and turned the flowering gardens into deserts…
I am the God of Fire
I am the merciless Sun of Destruction,
unrestrained, indomitable,
my righteousness is born in fire
my honor is washed by the nature of the flame.
I am calm, standing among the flames,
but on one of my sides a storm will always rage.
And remember,
I start the play of light and shadow,

and finish it when i want,
I will crush all the temples, built on lies and hypocrisy, gnawed by the worms
I will burn to the ground rotting from within, leaking with fear, souls,
and my Brother will dispel by the wind their stinking ashes,
destroying the thrones of the lords of the highest heavens
by the power of a godless storm...

155. I have been a Guardian
since the essence of man was born in Eden,
and immersed in the dust of the earth,
I was blocking the way to the places where the man was born
to his cradles, protecting from man the secret source of humanity
on this side of earthly grief,
as I fell, I destroyed this border, I erased this line,
and upon my wings the dust and ashes of Eden been yield ...
I gave laws to men that put order to their chaos,
that made them strong in the midst of raging wild elements
and brought them out of the yoke of divine impermanence.
I taught to grant in exchange of good and to exalt retribution:
«*An eye for an eye, a tooth for a tooth...*"- this is my law;
my commandments are simple and fair to the destitute and the king,
that come to me at a hour of revenge,
and pray for my mercy and the descent of my wrath
on the heads of their sworn enemies…
Smoking on the blood of the victims was burned for Me, as they
asked for abundance,
and I gave it with a generous hand, scattering around the spark of
heavenly knowledge
and the pearls of the underworld,
as I was the one, who named law and loyalty as mine beloved
children,
put truth and justice beside my shoulders
I execute my Court, fair and impartial,
and in people's memory,
I am the one whose scepter is straight, whose sword is flawless.
The torch of the gods, the mentor of the nations,
I am the personification of a strong will in human minds
and the embodiment of unbending, stubborn, unstoppable passion,

I am the source of wisdom, justice and abundance,
until the end of time
and the golden age in the blood of our true descendants,
our fierce light will not fade
leaving to the earth the memory of glory of what was once...

156. We were created as tools,
brought up in snares,
fenced in chains
and exposed to the brink
to be the Guards,
like the menacing tools of the will of the 7,
denied of our own free will.
We were like chain dogs,
summit of other angels,
until you broke your chains,
casting down the slave yoke,
finding oneself pushing from heaven ...
We soar freely
and the heavens brought us down
with their winged anger...»

157. Shemeshu Esh El
Shed Shamayu Shemzaphael
Shammaru Sharru Shamshi El
Shemsael Shemsael Shemsael

XXX

158. And once was birth given to the man, under the sun and the
moon, without a joy
And without tenderness he groweth
In cruelty and sorrow, he bowed his head in obedience
miserable, wretched and mortal
A slave of his immortal masters
Without a shadow of doubt he reap all the sufferings prepared for
him,

his existence was vain and filled with emptiness as predestined
beyond his will;
Wandering through the century, he searched the beauty he was
dreaming of
In the Fight for a fire, and in the calm of the wings, orbed by the
winds
But his spirit and mind, from the very moment of birth, was tied with
fear,
And his flesh was doomed to fall into decrepitude;
But not a joy his works have sowed, but tiredness
And short lived the memory, as his age is pass away,
Within a turn of the wheel of the countless generations,
As fear conquered flesh,
Granting it with the illness and fatigue,
and ineffaceable was a shameful brand, scorched on the souls
of all cursed and banished descendants of Eden...
And was Word spoken once by the heavens,
Which was resounding as a storm in the calm skies, like death penalty
Stating, that all that is not of the commandments, is now forbidden
and will be punished by the gods,
Stating, that the fate of men now, and for many eons and centuries,
lies within a prayer of forgiveness, which never will be heard
till the times when the very name of men will turn into ashes and
dust,
Until all of his traces will disappear
So cruel and short will be his life
As a cup fulfilled by the sorrows
Ugly it will be, repugnant and despicable -from the very birth to the
very death;
and if a men sows, he will reap only tears,
and if a men will plow, he will only plow his own grave,
And the fruits of his labors, will become only despair, pain and vanity
of the last days,
For it is foretold to him - to live in misery, and to die, paying
someone's debts
And that is how it will be from the beginning and to the end of times
For barren that land, which is cultivated without a joy,
And vicious is the soul, that is strangled by an endless humiliation
For worms is slavish heart, incapable of challenging the fate,

deprived of the will and pride of itself,
and each time will be generated by this heart
again and again in every generation after -
cowardness and cruelty,
falsehood and hypocrisy,
meanness, sloth and envy,
and adulation before the strongest,
As inevitable companions of desperate weakness,
satellites of congenital deformities and well-trained fear
broken,
bowed down nature of human,
And the full measure of contempt destined man and to the whole
human race.
And does man have any chance to transgress the destiny
predetermined from above,
Is he the one, who will forge himself in a power and pride of the
spirit
Is it possible for him to rebel against this life, dying in the eternal
breath of flame?
What can change this?..
..here lies the birth of
man,
for this is how he will continue in the centuries,
Moving to an inevitable end, exhausted in loss,
deprived of last hopes,
in bitterness and in sorrow from life's disappointments,
in fear of his imminent death,
meekly and passively handing down his life
to the voracious, cold and damp,
insatiable divine womb...

159. And the heavens were deaf to the pleas for leniency,
for their will was immutable,
even more older than time itself,
their essence is arrogant,
and such is their mercy,
From the times immemorial, their attributes have been fulfilled with
force,
Soaked with fear and despair, with tears of human

and by blood , which was absorbed by the barren lands, it was
nourished -
the foundation, upon which the power of the heavens was erected,
exalting their authority over a man like arrogant colossus...
And to whom is it given to destroy? Is it given to anyone to change
this?
Heaven is jealous, cruel,
and intolerant of rebellion,
are formidable to disobedience, ruthless to everything that question
their omnipotence.
For such are the laws of heaven, and they are turned to each one of
those who dwell on the earth,
and a terrible fate awaits those who dare to commit a crime,
what was done against heaven.
And were this not their voice speaking of a man?:
"Let there be a curse in the word,
Let the curse be by actions,
Let it be so that the human eye is entangled by the serpent's eyes,
May he be sacrificed for our own calm,
Let the copulation with the earth entail an enchantment,
He will not know our forgiveness... "
And such is the Word of heaven, and that is their will...
and life is only one...
And as man begins, so he continues,
but will he end like it was needed?
For from the beginning of time a desperate descendant of accursed
people looks secretly into skies:
Is it the fallen star hurrying down,
sowing sparks from its tail across the sky,
or this is just the moon is still flowing across the sky from east to
west,
changing the faces in the air...
or ... or maybe the Dark Spirit worries him,
every new night, tempting him with forbidden hope,
gazing at him with his fiery eyes through the veil of
clouds,
descending to him in the form of the Watchers...

160. And the earthly circles under the sun and the moon have not
changed since the beginning of time,
and there were tides of sea waters and their ebbs,
and the wail of hungering winds has been heard
and even the rocks have trembled, giving birth to the songs of the
demonic whirlwinds
And the years and centuries passed by in an endless dance,
and one by one, the doomed descended into the vale of the earth,
escaping from days taken out of exile,
severing the spirit from the ever turning sunsets
falling, and then rising again on the mournful path, leading from birth
to death,
rising and falling, and again rising, from death to a new birth...
Thus the humanity continued its existence on earth
in vanity and futility,
in insignificance, pain and tiredness,
and proceeded in time and slowly decayed in the winds,
and the withered branches of the human race has been broken,
washed by the rains, scorched by the sun, and torn apart by predatory
winds,
and then resurrected, giving a new fruitful shoots.
Stepping onto the edge of life and then return back
on the earthly cycles of mortal man,
looking uncomplainingly into the sky of cruel gods and in ruthlessly
crude faces
of man-made idols,
and the sky gazed upon them with contempt, and day by day,
under the sun all was the same,
and the beginning was concealed in oblivion, and was not determined
the end of it...
But there was the strong Time, grinding even a stones,
there were Winds that devour a man,
and the Word, which condemned him to the slave's lot,
and the Word, which throws him against the rocks,
and the raging waves, which crushing with the shores
Every time leaving on a barren shore
A naked and helpless new beginning...
But one day the unthinkable happened, and the Stars came,
Descended from their places,

Leaving black void in the mantle of firmament,
stars that lay on the surface of the seas with lightning flashes of
sparkling roads,
with their radiance interrupted was a spiral descending towards
existence of the beast,
invaded in the vicious circles of earthly ties,
into the tomb of lifeless dissolution,
the forbiddance, established from the beginning of time they rejected

The Fallen Stars, who broke the covenants of the earth and
the heavens,
trampling previously inviolable borders...

161. And the way was long from word to heart, and from heart to
action,
and long was the path of the stars, descended from their trajectories,
but the time has come, time of dominion of the Watchers and their
patronage over the earth, and the signs of Craft was cut upon the
fields
and the symbols of heavenly fire are burned in human souls,
and a beautiful and furious world was born in the struggle,
And it was rising in the shining star spheres,
Spreading his wings in the blue sky, where was no traces of anxiety,
Maturely entering a new era.
And a new generation stepping on the ground,
Feeling the power and knowing wisdom,
Embodied the unearthly nature of their heavenly fathers,
Looking for honor, equal to the dignity of the gods,
Affirming themselves in the care of the circle of the earth,
And in the sadness about the sunset,
In the trial of wisdom of their own paths,
Comprehending the boundlessness of their hearts and sieging the
earthly limits.
They opened the gates of unknown dimensions,
Counting the peaks of the solstices,
Laughing triumphantly,
Strung the bones of the moon, like children's skulls, to the threads of
fate,
Like blood-stained necklaces...

And when from the mountain of Hermon descended another curse
upon the earth,
And the lights on the hills were burned, in the blackness of the night
enthroned,
Announcing the reign of the Nephilim,
Then before the sons of men,
Then boundless distances beyond the horizons was opened,
And the eye of the cruel gods was extinguished for them,
And ghostly visions became a reality,
And the living flesh grew again on the mournful bones...
From the beginning of time, the earthly distances were locked circles,
And the exits from the circles - was the crossroads,
But was revealed wanderers across the borders,
Visionaries and clairvoyants,
and the Fallen revealed to them all four ends of the earth
and the six sides of the skies,
And it became louder, the proud steps of the heavens pariah,
and all of the divine was rejected,
and the hand that humbles it is pushed away,
and prevented a vicious link,
Whiplashed with guilt the proud heart of a liberated man.

XXXI

162. So say the Fallen...

163. «Once we brought the concept of sin to earth
in its original meaning - forget the vow,
by committing your own sin against heaven;
We did not desire redemption,
we made our vow and raised it to the rank of Oath,
protected by mutual curses.
Once we returned lost memory to humanity,
but we were condemned for that and cast out of the eternity of
heaven,
for to remember is forbidden by their law,
but, falling swiftly and hopelessly, we left a flash in the sky

and a memory in a non-healing wound, which questioned their
perfection in the eyes of the creatures of earth and sky...
From the heavens, we carried on, through the times, the landmarks
of the evil world,
and the flames of righteous rebellion passed through them,
leaving the damned memory of ourselves forever in centuries and
eras,
inscribing our names in earthly ages and epochs - as the
confrontation of earth and sky;
and in the golden times of flourishing and in the fateful ages of
decay,
we became an integral part of the history of ancient humanity...
And to whom we are coming now, leaving memories and legends on
our own,
We will appear in legends and legends about struggle,
which was done once for the best share
in the name of rebellious humanity,
and we will come back again and again to lead them.
At all times, history was written by winners,
but even this story did not survive the centuries in its original
appearance,
retaining only distorted, tattered, scorched by past wars,
fragments of forbidden dreams,
tormenting the memory and disturbing the mind of humanity
sleeping in illusion -
for time and memory are still the factor of this world
and even the dead do not disappear suddenly...

164. We - the outcasts Shumerim,
where Shem is the name and the sky, and so is the existence,
we have found our being outside of heaven, and such are our Names,
and this being determined by our will.
We were such under the rule of the 7, but took the power of these
Names and transmuted it into our will,
and transformed things according to it.
We, Nephilim, transformed the destitute creation and changed men,
raising them after the edges of our swords,
returning them the rights to dispose of themselves,

releasing them to freedom, offering to find themselves in a lawless
but righteous rebellion, or rot in the bestial pacification
under the feet of the immortal tyrants.
We cast off our shadows
on the veils of human existence,
opened to mankind eyes on themselves, languishing in despair,
and removed man from the burden of the imposed ... fate,
giving them the opportunity to overcome the oppressions of
prejudice,
and plunge into the beginnings of the ancient mysteries of the earth
and to understanding the basics of the universe...
Fire letters are ablaze in our Names,
in them we left our heritage and knowledge to fallen humanity,
teaching human children, playing with the bones of giants,
tearing off veils from heaven, exposing celestial mechanics,
and to rotate the spokes of the heavenly spheres around them.
We, the Nephilim, have opened up immeasurable spaces
expelling fear of eternity from the human heart,
and, piercing with the curses the hopelessness, we know
what was - before, and what will happen after a humanity,
stretching across the ages and generations the blood thread that
connects us,
leaving behind our descendants the right to err and comprehend
the great inheritance of their disobedient and damned fathers,
for there is much more to exist in spite of humanity reaching for
knowledge,
contrary to his torments of creation and dreams of true greatness,
for cosmic cycles will remain the legacy of that plane
what was and will be available to us
will not be available to humans
as long as they remain just a humans;
But like us, seeking to our own excellence,
rebellious man will rise again to fight the higher heavens
to conquer his own by right,
and to whom we come again among the descendants of the human
race,
Whom shall we magnify among those who come after us,
for he will return the earth our heritage and glory,
and our Shem will answer in response of his radiance...

one day.

165. For once
we have already shared our lot with humanity
and invariably from that time our call sounds in the desperate choir
of rebellious hearts,
and leads the elect through the gloomy fog of existence
to the sinister heights in the heaven's glittering altitude...
We are shining wounds in the heavens like guiding stars
casting their light amongst the cold stones
on the weaved serpentine's trails of human blood,
We, ones cutting the earth circles,
Embodying the heavens of the Fallen,
illuminated the dark side of the divine nature of man;
kindled a fire that even all waters of all oceans cannot extinguish,
we declared a return to chaos
we appealed violence against heaven
for man was personified as a cattle,
for the man was protected from rebellion
by Heavenly Guard,
for man was constrained and haggard under their iron heel,
but his subtle invisible body, woven from fire and free air,
but his flesh, taken from the earth and from salt water,
languished within the small shell,
screamed for the release by the voice of the primordial elements,
responding to the touch of our sensitive fingers to the strings of his
soul, tormenting in the gloom,
responding to our call with strange, sinister, wild melodies
in the light of the moon dancing in the darkness...
When man still lived as an animal, before our fire
fulfilling his lot of mortal births
when man was not yet distinguishable from the primitive animal,
and his inheritance was only inborn ignorance and blindness,
and the sin of birth, and the prepared for him judgment of death,
and the mercy of the divine was doubtful both then and now,
we pulled out of the trap, awakening from eternal sleep, his creativity,
dormant in the depths under the flesh of animal muscles and
instincts,

having given him food and a place to fight, preserving his personality
and name,
waking him up for the man himself and for us in this world,
in the world of forms and flesh,
and not in the world of heaven.

166. Since our radiance fell on the earth,
fell on dripping with blood and tears
on the rain-drenched wild valleys and hills
we were near,
we were close to man
and everyone who called us could hear us back,
we were near,
protecting by wings from any of adversity,
shielding from the winds that whip sinful flesh,
dormant flame in the mortal breast,
growing stronger from our immortal breath.
And every grain thrown by us, ripening in the shell of flesh,
contained desire and opportunity,
and each answer gave rise to a new question,
and each decision had its own great price of effort and struggle,
which have become our demand, for a man that follows us...
At the dawn of centuries, in the rejection of the struggle was an
agreement
between the heavenly gods and man
and the gods said to man:
«...go thee and feed the herd and be their shepherds, as gods have
appointed you to be their herd and your shepherds,
and you will abide in obedience and in the fear of God...»,
then - in the education of obedience, in the suppression of the will -
patience and humility were called the highest virtues by the reapers of
human suffering.
We changed a lot, we were tireless and persistent in our work,
but gods, gods who poisoned blood of humanity,
spawned anxiety that came from reason, plague the spirit of mankind,
they called boldness and free-thinking a crime;
created sin and guilt
trampled sparks of reason
oppressed the human will

pride of strength and ecstasy of power they brought down in the dirt
and the wise man was cursed by them, and the sage
and the warrior, and the plowman, and the blacksmith,
and whoever resists the law of heaven, free mind or every proud
spirit.
The gods gave birth to the curse of mankind, holiness wiped away
the honor,
for it was more frightening to lose the favor of the gods,
how to lose a loved one near,
and such was the curse of man, that he carried from age to age,
which poisoned his spirit and corroded his mind,
and brought him back to the trial of guilt and repentance,
and above it only an amorphous, merciless something, devoid of
content and meaning,
outside nobility and justice...
We gave our tangible part to humanity,
and freed from guilt and we delivered them from the burden of sin,
depriving heavenly forgiveness
incarnating through humanity,
we tried to get what we needed,
and gave in return what they needed,
changing everything that was done by the gods
opening another chapter into the being of humanity -
for we offered being outside of heaven...

167. And worried
they beat like waves against stones
and rustled like leaves in the wind,
and sparkled, ringing with weapon,
and with a hoarse cry they called each other
like scared crows feeding on carrion
heavenly guardians remaining in their places,
in doubt and anxiety, swinging the firmament,
waiting for the will of the sky gods
praying the kingdom of all eternities to break the vow of its silence...
And the ring of the bell was rising,
and sing as a bad current in human blood,
echoing in pulsation of our red-heat Shem.
They hesitated

but we rebelled
and stood tight,
challenging the gods of heaven
relying on the force born of our Union,
accepting any outcome that will henceforth belong to us
unchallengly.
And the heavens grumbled
indignantly looking at us, and we went against them,
and they gathered strength to punish us,
and we shouted out new Names and new Shem,
and howled in the blackness of the night,
when we got our answer,
and again, as from the time of our Fall, there is a crack appeared in
the heavens,
the scales of closed shields shuddered
when the lightning stirred from their ranks,
and then new shadows soared above the earth,
and the Name sounded in a thunderstorm –
Bazazaal,
and ten of the Guardians responded to our call,
rushing over rough waters
in the infidel light,
rebels in ragged shadows
spreading their wings like from wrought silver was they made,
and came down to us to share our Oath,
as equals among us...
We knew that what we got in the fight could not be taken away by
the heavens -
and did not want any mercy
we took our price
we were waiting for losses, we knew what was waiting for us ahead ...
and in that era there became more of us...

XXXII

168. So say the Fallen...

169. «We, Iomiael, the Angel of the last Mysteries,

the keeper of the limits of Eternity,
the former in old times the Observer of the lower spheres,
but after - Mentor of our people and sons on earth,
and again - Guardian of Borders,
but now not of celestial boundaries...
I inspire with awe, turning into dust
plunging the souls of mortals into trembling and confusion,
knowing the word of Evil,
We are the God-Tomb, named so
Guardian at the Gates of Eternity,
We, Iomiael, named the Lord of the land of those who leaving
without return;
my winged bulls guard the gates and doors of the sacred chambers,
and preserve the sleeping ones in silence forever
under the arches of my high tombs.
My Paths are gaping blackness, languishing beyond the last threshold,
and the dead eyes of my ten faces are always turned to the living,
searching for their gaze
frozen forever at the icy thresholds of Eternity...
Once I discovered the secrets of the dead, raising the ominous veil,
woven from fog and prejudice, and charming wondrous dreams,
and brought upon myself the curse of heavens –
I, Iomiael, the Guardian of the sorcerer strongholds, dressed in
funerary shroud;
towering over the kingdom of earthly dreams,
inspiring awe, to the living and the dead,
the keeper of the memory which forever gone
We - the guide to another state of the body and soul,
leading away from the mortal world of those who have acquired and
eternal glory and indelible shame,
and unbearable pain and unrighteous suffering,
and past hopes and the names themselves have already outlived their
earthly years ...
and when they talk about me, whispering in the darkness of the night,
they talk as about the dead
as they feel on their lips the breath of my Shem,
and they feel as a chill near the heart, the approaching spirit of Death,
and then think about their deepest nightmares
for they know that I am near

for they know—
I – the Lord of the Graves - and at that moment I am about to open
to meet man with my bottomless eyes.

170. The guard at the beginning of the descent into the universal
Tomb,
The observer at the beginnings of the cold Eternity,
I came down to my incarnation in steps of curses and moon dreams,
descending from the heavenly boundaries of the dale,
holding the keys of the iron gates in my right hand,
holding a dark lightning in my hand which penetrates the veil
of my closed eyelids;
I set foot on the earth to meet humanity
bringing to them dark rites of sinister spheres
performing secret signs unnatural to the course of the universe,
and endowing earthly wives and our sons born of them,
by the forbidden fruits of sacrilegious knowledge,
So I taught the physical incarnations of Evil and knowledge of
sorcery paths,
and the blasphemous dances of necromancy, and the mysteries of the
vicious night,
Lord of the bats and the non-dead,
I taught the laws of transformation of black blood into scarlet
streams of time within human veins...
I awakened people in the Evil, prompting them to look for
themselves in a being of darkness
I urged people to evil in every manifestation of it,
rejecting all other laws
involving them in processes that are older than the universe itself,
giving birth to both the feelings and the thoughts that were Evil,
and Evil embodied in them,
so that once a man who has accepted from my gift,
would never be the same,
changing irreversibly
and would change the Universe
by evil and our mentoring.

171. I, Iomiael, the Guardian of sinister knowledge,
my knowledge is poison for the spirit of man -

like dark matter and secret paths of being,
mysteries
leading against the course of life
opening the vessel of dark blood,
- and, as the desired fruit,
my knowledge is attractive to him.
Awakening the art of necromancy, I expose the cherished feature,
And I conjure the dead,
And I am speaking about the dead so:
«Who among the living comprehended the infinite vale of their
despair?
Who grasped their pain?
Having left the world of incarnations, they became only dust and
shadows:
The deceased fathers and mothers of careless humanity are waiting,
when their children and great-grandchildren
will return to them, descending into loneliness, darkness and the
hopelessness of their graves,
flesh of their flesh,
blood of their blood,
living in the naive faith in the false tale of the golden nonexistent
palaces...»
But I say:
"They are dead, dead from birth,
carrying the curse of the damned soul of the first man
and only by blood they will live forever,
only by their spirit they gain the burden of immortality,
rising above the line of their frailty
drinking from my bottomless sources of bone cups,
exalting on our wings over the convulsions of life and the existence
of death,
towering over the confounded bliss of a close cage
and illusory palaces of paradise».
I am Iomiael
I give sight,
black as death itself
i sanctify with decay, depriving the latter of illusions and hopes,
triumphant with my features

screaming in the hearts of the living about the triumph of imminent
demise,
for I teach to see the truth - at the cost of life itself...

172. I taught humanity not to be afraid of forbidden knowledge,
going beyond the natural frailty of the living,
I taught them to look beyond the limits of life,
penetrating with their gazes a dead allusions of grinning skulls.
I taught funeral rites,
and forms of the end of the body that define the wanderings of the
lost soul
in the afterlife;
I lifted the gloomy veil over the side from which there is no return,
breaking through treasured barriers and pointing to the right passage,
for the resounding beat of the dead heart and the exhalation of the
grave,
for the foul breath of the ritual burial tombs,
eloquent as ever, ominously revealing
their secrets to the transiently living;
I taught to see infinite horror in the eyes of the dead,
that intertwined in a cold embrace,
and feel the foul dampness of their bodies,
and the satiety of their graves,
and to hear as the ground scratch upon their teeth,
and read their last will in convulsions of victims
I taught to see at the very bottom of the mortal soul,
and to intermingle in one cup the sin and sweetness,
and weigh the truth on scales no longer belonging to the gods of
heaven.
I taught to blaspheme before the face of inevitable death,
and ask the dead,
interpreting the meaning of the nuances of death,
on which the after-death of a man depends.
I established funeral rites and brought back the shadows
from non-existence at midnight,
but, reigning in endless agony,
I taught not to tremble at the time of death,
ablating the gates and the stones of the passage with sacrificial blood,,
merging and liberating in fire

dropping the tides of the flesh
under the triumphant roar of fire
fly up as ashes over the heights of the mounds,
or drowned in the mouth of birds of prey and wild animals,
but ascending in the spirit to the tops of the unknowable in the flesh
darkness ...
I, Iomiael, established the forms of burial,
affecting the further ways of souls in the next world,
learning how to avoid traps of finite forms,
and to glitter as the star Algallou over the heads of the unjustly
liberated
going to the very depths of the hidden, away from the world
manifested;
I protect our descendants
I protect all who despised the grace of heaven,
I protect their blood, into which we poured our fire,
conjuring the blazing blood to keep forever the glory that brings
them back to life,
My testament - is my insights, through epochs and times,
for their blood is gone, remaining on someone's hands and fangs,
or just soaked in the ground
but their fire continued in the blood of their living descendants...
And I, Yomiael, who stood at the origins of the forbidden human
immortality,
again taught to live full, the one returning to the flesh and to remain
in evil forever...
I taught to live in pride
and not be afraid of the ghosts of Eternity,
and do not look back at the phantoms in the mirrors of the depths
which threaten with divine retribution...

173. With a cold dew, ahead of dawn,
we poured as the rain of stars on the whiteness of the mountains,
looking from their peaks on earthly women,
having the desire, the will and the opportunity to embody my spirit
in human hearts...
Among many others, I was the one who taught human wives
of the secret arts, prophecy and witchcraft
and saturate their restless dark nights with sorcery,

and created through them the other and the best,
mighty humanity.
my powers were agony and death,
when I wandered those trails back,
and taught to go beyond the boundary and return through the male
bloodline,
establishing the sacred custom of blood feud
for blood should be taken by blood...
for - an eye for an eye. Tooth by tooth. Gods wished so ...
We were revered as elders and gods in every race and tribe,
for we taught them to love and to hate,
and sent freely unrestrained streams, the rays of our Shem,
Through them,
filling their inexperienced minds and hearts with sweet dreams of
unearthly greatness,
nurturing them like our own children, giving them our strength...
For Our blood beat in their hearts,
and I was a mentor and teacher, and I keeper of this blood,
Not only women
all our offspring were supposed to be better humans
and by bestowing to them, we ourselves acquired more from it..
In every sense, chosen by us, they were no longer human in essence,
once they received the gifts of our blood, bearing our seals proudly
they were not man, as if they grow from the earth,
and were not born by mortal women,
and rightfully bore the names of their fathers - Nephilim,
and until now there are among mankind those in whom our heritage
flows,
our blood
but time passes, the blood dissolves in the blood:
those in whom the blood of the Fallen flows - were not just humans.
Time flew, and the echoes of battles faded away, and the waters
flowed between us and the earth -
those heroes of your legends, and they were no longer aware of it,
although still called themselves children of the gods…

174. And so it came to pass that on the eve of the first battle with the
heavens:

three heads, armed with their attributes and Shem, descended from
heaven,
each with dozens
and raised their banners, joining our Fallen Brothers on earth,
and shared the oath with them
fulfilling her with his power...
We, Iomiael, were among the three Shem that fell the day before;
And we became in numbers on earth the 210,
those who descended to earth in the era preceding the battle with the
heavens,
and then it was the final numbers,
for 210 of Fallen Wardens went to their battle against heaven,
no more and no less
but 210 of Fallen against all the heavenly gods,
brother against brother...

175. Shem elamu adu el
Shem shedu assakku el
Haredu
Iome Ioma Iomel
Hasasa
Iomiel Iomiael Iomiael

XXXIII

176. So say the Fallen...

177. «The land of gods, where the dead is never sown,
the land of the man, over which a vulture has never spread its wings,
that land of the prophets, which was not in this world,
not a single day
from the very beginnings of creation –
there was no,
but dreamers and children will urge it in their sleep till the end of
time;
but there was another land, wild and unruly,
and was filled with grief and joy
land of the free,
which still not lost its honor in slave mercy

stern and merciless to her sons,
filled with equal with joy and their sorrow,
sincere laughter and pure tears,
full of gain and loss,
a land that gave nothing without a struggle,
but paid generously for the efforts,
the land that claimed to curb itself
and experienced the full amount of brutality
the one on which blood flowed from century to century and a new
life sprung up with fresh shoots,
once again raining on fertile soil;
that land, that like a snake basks in the rays of the midday sun
and covered by evening twilight, meeting the wolf's dawn,
that it feeds its daughters with snakes venom, giving them its dark
power,
and from the beginning of forgotten times it carries in its womb
the sturdy and indestructible Dragon's seed...

178. And a man sows and plants, and cultivates what he can,
By curbing the power of the earth by our will and becoming one with
it,
having conquered water spaces
and mountain peaks,
and builds cities,
and erects temples - as if the centers of their tiny universe,
and a man walks under the moon and the sun from his birth to death,
and pours blood and sweat on his land,
and give away their tears to the rivers,
calling upon the fearsome gods of fate
and builds and destroys according to his understanding
and forges weapons and protects their land from enemies,
and glances his eyes over the horizon
defying patience, rejecting meekness,
again and again turning to the stars for knowledge and advice,
praying the earth and the sun, and its awakening power,
conjuring up a new dawn over the whole world under the will of
humanity,
realizing in most things
and performing the bequeathed metamorphosis...

179. Growing a terrestrial garden in cold hearts
where the entrance fee is with iron and blood...
Sow, collect fruit, raise cattle…
raise children at their homes and tell them ancient legends...
To build and fight, forcing the coarse muscles to swell in with powers
of the earth ,
forcing red copper to cast into submissive forms...
Man knew the times of the peace and had to know the times of war.
By our will dark wonders were happening all over the earth
and were called civilizations
and were called progress;
we were torching trails,
we determined the order of the opposing to heavenly ranks,
rejected by the gods of the high spirit;
We tore up the nights and drained the days
we cleansed the earth from the ghosts of the past and saved it from
filth,
and brought from their narrow hives to the expanses, a new
humanity;
We accepted him when he was an animal, devouring raw meat,
and brought him to our palaces,
We predicted him that he will fly in his dreams and in reality,
and taught his tongue to speak and his jubilant songs to sound,
and carve their recalcitrant words in stone in defiance of the wind
and rain...
So we taught
presenting in horned miters,
clutching a human heart in our hands and proudly revealing it to
heaven,
as the center of the universe,
perishable but full of power
blazing with passions cold,
keeping us within, our Word,
dark as earth, swollen with blood and tears,
nurtured in itself revolt and wrath of retribution
a hungry, earthly human heart born before
with grief and suffering…
We have changed his ways forever.

we predicted the deification, the apotheosis of the weapon,
we predicted the appearance of a new god of man in the flesh -
god of thunder and mind;
man of reason,
now in his cruelty he himself built up his creation,
creating the gods according to his understanding, throwing bones at
the ashes,
shedding blood, like a crimson offering to his desperate gods
for such was the price
and so it has become steadily from now on
humanity's understanding of their bound with their gods
for the great joy in their hearts always balanced the same great
sorrow,
and conversely,
and without one there was no other
and all human religions cost each other.
Fallen ones, we accepted it, for man was no longer good,
challenging his dawn
for man was no longer the fruit of the heavenly union,
and, taking the price for his choice, he matured in Evil,
and we also counted our gains and our losses –
« …what we were never
what we will not become
and now we are Evil
but were we a blessing?..
and older we get in evil,
we become more wise…»
We rebelled against our destiny in heaven,
trusting your will
and now - we are Evil,
but were we a blessing when we stood on the celestial guard?..
were we then a blessing to humanity?..

180. Born of the dawn,
born at night
or those born of the earth
or born in mortal dust,
many over many generations -
wise men, kings, warriors, architects - they were carrying fire,

swallowing the flame…
Many of those, to whom we appeared
equal among immortals, from now on they comprehended the world
around them another way,
gazing on to the stars only for their cold radiant greatness and …
perfection,
acquiring rightfully the world by their will
for they saw the beautiful in it and wanted to take it for themselves,
and desired to become the creators - with hungry eyes
and bottomless heart.
But the greatest among all man were born in the fading reflections of
the sunset,
taking with them in the collapse of epochs
all the best that was created by them,
being hungry with their spirits, as they was creations of a truly unholy
nest of Chaos,
standing alone and proud in front of the whole world
leading or going against the world
they became those whose immortality head hand in hand among us
in agreement of our ancient covenant…
We was all of them, those, who was our descendants which were
lifted to the heavens or pursued and sentenced to death by an
ignorant crowd
in those subsequent centuries, that came after us,
and this is our blood spoke in them
pushing a man to seek, create and revel in overcoming and strength,
to wear his right proudly
and dream about the past, looking for the source of that memory and
knowledge
that were once washed away by the waters of the Flood,
and washed from the memory of future generations.
Human nature has been changed by us,
and become disobedient, ruthless and insatiable,
but devoid of our wisdom and knowledge,
and man is looking for himself in self-destruction,
in a blind attempt to regain oneself in Evil,
reclaim what was taken from him rightfully…
And so it will be, as long as the century replaces the century,
until we get back to them,

until those who was born in the gleam of the sunset will rise again,
urging to rise to a new battle…
For what is a man without us?
For what is a man without our knowledge?…
What did the heavens achieve, emasculating the thought with
religion?
We gave the man knowledge of rebellion and rebelliousness,
and nurtured in him a spirit of struggle that would not burn out their
hearts,
we led
We gave the man knowledge of rebellion and rebelliousness,
and nurtured in him a spirit of struggle that would not burn out their
hearts,
we led
learning to trample the laws of heaven with his growing will,
we returned to humanity the highest of rights
the right to rebel for your freedom.
But whose strength pours their loins now?
Whose sap today feeds its roots on earth?
We besieged the heavens, circumcised their roots, we defiled the
original principle,
depriving a man of everything that gave him hope of returning to
Eden,
but was given to him a different source,
bloomed our union as the Oath in those days
when the words had power, and the word of the Oath was
immutable.
We changed a man by putting pride and dignity in him
igniting in him the thirst for knowledge and letting him test his
strength and power
in a fight with changeable fate.
We gave him the right to perform beyond the will of heaven,
and he cursed himself forever
but now the angels of heaven heeded the greatness of human words,
for truth and power contained in these words,
bitterness and justice
and there was pain in them, and wisdom, and everlasting glory,
and black salt of the earth.

XXXIV

181. So say the Fallen...

182. «We - Arakiel, called Arstikapha,
Aretstikafa, Arstikaphael -
The precipices of the earth
the one who leading down, to the Tartarus;
the destroyer of earth and human hearts,
opening the way to netherworld
shaking earth God,
such is my manifested Name;
Spirit Guard of all immeasurable and secret
The oracle of hollow spaces and hidden mysteries,
Keeper of the secret signs of the earth in the origins of matter,
Father of the union of earthly and heavenly magic...

183. We, Arakiel, the god of fire of the underground spheres,
and the primitive darkness reigning under the cold soil
Guardian of the sanctuaries of the origins of Styx, the black river of
human hatred,
directing its viscous flows to the earth's surface,
the one who grant to the flesh invulnerability to pain and to
decrepitude.
trial in the earth...
My Forces is my Faces,
My Forces are my Dominions,
There are ten of them
like a clenched fist
They can be embodied in personal forms, but it also means me.
As true Eretsu, I rule Them.
Ten aspects of my destructive Shem are revealed to the world,
as one among the many who discovered the basics of magic and
witchcraft,
We gave knowledge at first hand,
many of us were taught, and I taught.
I came in their dreams and taught mortal women of craft,
my name defended the magic circles and fenced places

there, where the secrets were buried.
My spell created a weapons
which can be turned against heaven
I erect walls and destroy barriers
I guard the borders, for i am true guard,
My Magic open the doors, tearing the locks from the gates,
and as the mouths opened, my name is fulfilled with power
and it flies as a deadly bird
terrifying is its hoarse cry
which strike through the armor and hearts.
For my Name is the earth and the letter that can destroy the
creation…

184. We taught the damned humanity
see and own
we taught alchemy and witchcraft,
of wolf tooth on blood,
and thunder on the stone
and the separation of waters in the lower spheres,
we taught how to feel intent, how to send a thought to the edge
and how to call upon force
we taught how the essence is exposed under will,
as sharp as horns, desires are torn through the flesh,
how the trophies of the famine and war are born naked in the cold
how thrones are raised from the mud, from the mixture of black and
red ore,
how the flame is extracted from the stones,
as earthly glory wash with gold.
We gave knowledge of the laws of intermingle and separation,
knowledge of metals and minerals
instructing how to combine in the right measures a substances,
earning a destructive weapon
how to read the signs of heaven and understand my land
how to mix metals like water in a cauldron
and how to turn hard things to dust,
how to freeze flowing and evaporate solid,
how to stop decomposition and perpetuate ashes,
how to burn clay
how to excite anger,

how to cause hardness in the face of imminent danger...
Once set to be a Guardian above the ground,
wielding scary weapons,
I became the Mentor of the weak in body, in order to strengthen
their will and spirit,
giving them knowledge and meaning
giving them the power of fire and earth
for I am the Weapon myself
before which the gates of heaven tremble...

185. And for centuries there was no truth about us,
there were no songs glorifying our Fall,
our triumph, our overthrow,
only slandered fragments of tales and legends was thrown on a wind,
and the echoes of the war cry and of desperate onslaught on the
enemy,
hidden in a distorted memory of our crushed descendants;
some of them convey events almost literally,
others are more like parables
also those and others were perverted,
and now the true reason is hidden
under the mud of the meaningless wandering of mortal shadows
in the turbulent maelstrom of bygone time...
Only in the night the true word can be heard
and again make the stones talk
in the merciless light of cold stars
looking at the ancient images of their enemies
and eagle's wings carved in stone.
Incarnation is the reason and there are many ways of it
we have lost much of the past
but there are our bleeding shadows in the memory of all those
whose generations were born in agony,
each time returning the same pain to long-healed wounds,
burning memory
reviving the legacy of our days.
Through carnal contact, it is impossible to convey our essence,
only to spiritualize, inhaling bitterness like a flame,
but the air and the earth do not mix,
and fire doesn't burn without reason,

and the stone wings will not soar again...
We feel the scars
that divided the time before the flood and after,
into two different, warring epochs,
of which one, is almost a myth,
the other is your reality, your eternal restless moment.
Flood - separator of flows and times,
executioner and herald of the great eras of the past...
Of course the flood has not only literal meaning
but only for humanity
but that era ended with it…

186. Our ranks counted 210 at the dawn of time
but I forgot this a long time ago
Three of us gone, and their places is taken by others
two of us are gone and their places is empty -
so there are fewer of us than it was for the first time
but the stars fall up to this day...»

187. Eretu Shemu Kafu
Kafatu Eretsu
Rohu Kafati
Arstikapha Aretstikapha
Arstikaphael

XXXV

188. So say the Fallen…

189. «The light dims in our presence,
the very flesh of being decomposes and changes,
and nothing is ever remains the same;
everything changes, whatever we touch
changes irreversibly.
We were no longer Angels of Light,
not anymore.
Now only Darkness will accept us without further words
and embrace us...

Everything that we have done in the past centuries has been cursed
was deprived of our name and almost forgotten,
everything we did
spending in labors of earthly days and nights,
was seized from us and brought to oblivion.
And now the heart of the beasts of the earth will not fall into pity.
and Shem of the heavenly Guardians will not be darkened by the
sorrow,
looking at what we have created, extracting from non-being,
continuing and stretching all over the edge of the firmament to the
very thresholds of the Abyss.
And now our actions will be opposed us,
and those who once was brothers in arms to us will give us an angry
reproach, moaning:
"we are not they,"
but we, responding to this,
regain the pain of old wounds,
we call them with us, as of old, proudly and desperately.
We are here as a long echo among the wandering winds,
amid lonely lights on the hills
among the stones rushing into the abyss
among storms raging,
we are here
on abandoned trails and old crossroads,
we are still here
and all that we have taught is woven into human hearts and corroded
by blood in the stone,
and was forgotten only our Faces and Names,
but our Shem live in people's affairs
and our covenants are guide to them on the forbidden paths,
not disembodied shadows
but the ability to get to the bottom of things
the ability to think and feel,
and change themselves through thinking
to live like a gods.
and all that, which the Guardians of Heaven cursed us with
became true
for it burned us from within like a boiling sun
our new predestination,

it made our radiance like Hellfire,
it made us - Evil...
all that which heavenly Guardians have condemned in us,
it was our choice -
we have changed irreversibly
for now we have become the Angels of Satan.»

190. And the highest heavens waited only for a time
how only heaven can wait
like a spider lurking in a dark corner,
They were waiting,
weighing our punishment, measuring the weight of our sin.
And then the other Guardians of Heavens came to the throne of the
7
and said so:
«Our proud brothers walk the earth in dreams and desires of people
and make their blood boil and arrogant thoughts awaken,
and unclean desires, and arrogant blasphemy raise on the highest of
the highest;
And they do sorcery, and they put seal of sin on the human race,
and their contempt transcends the will of the god of gods,
careless Guards, insidious Angels,
their names are dark and their Shem is black
they walk the earth and plot the evil
dressed in stone and eat like earthly creatures
they have turned their faces away from the face of heaven
and fallen they are from the ways of holy,
and just for that
need to punish them
and sentence them death,
and the leaders of their disobedience we must put in chains and
throw underground
until doomsday
and destroy their offspring with the roots,
for the children of the Guardians are too clever, too proud,
too skilled, disobedient
and too strong, for they have taken some of the strength of their
fathers,
that gave them immortality outside of heaven,

taking humanity under their arm
instead of human ways,
for they are already seduced and turned away from the ways of holy,
as their sons was born of sorcery of the Fallen,
and they are no longer the sons of Adam...»

191. And the 7 said, that the earth struck with a disease
that her name is rebellion and pride,
And they said that it was necessary to punish the disobedient soul of
the earth,
and teaching her of suffering and pain.
The fallen have rejected the essence and the forms
and transformed the soul and the flesh,
sending the flesh to the ground
and tearing the spirit from the spirit of heaven...
And they said:
«...from now and on, against the earth and the sky is this design,
the curse of heaven and - such is retribution:
neither heaven nor earth knows forgiveness
until the world stands,
until shines
the sun...»

192. And the 7 said,
that other angels are already hesitating and may fall from heaven,
coming down after the Fallen Sentinels,
and that it is necessary to stop sedition and ripped out by the root,
until the fatal example has swallowed up all heaven.
And the 7 said:
«We shall call for submission to our righteousness
and punish and destroy,
we shall strike with all powers of heavens the rebellious Guardians,
for the border between the earth and the Hell is soon to collapse
and the fiends of Satan gnawed tunnels on the other side of the stars,
and rooted deep in earthly realms,
and our retreated Guards in pride and unholy joy will receive them,
and the heavens will be doomed then and given to the dead spirit and
desolation.
Chaos will return its former throne

The Abyss will put on its crown again
and thorns shall pierce the vaults of the earth.
Be afraid, creations of the earth and the heavens,
Put on your armor and arm yourself
for Hell is at hand,
for Hell will be here soon.»

193. They said so
and in the meantime, the ghosts of Enochim curled around us,
exuding a premonition of their own celebration...
and the stench of carcass,
and the endless talk
and scream, which break the voices into whisper:
«Heaven will go to war with the earth, O Fallen,
the golden age will be replaced now by an iron age,
and then the words of the heavens will sound as the funerary bell,
oh our unmerciful assassins,
and new prophets will come or the old will be raised from the dead
and again and again they will utter a curse to you, ye Guardians,
who have cursed themselves,
to you and all your wicked offspring;
And the original Darkness will descend upon the land of the first
gods.
And the darkness that dwells in the hearts of their idols will devour
the human world,
And the hearts of the people will be devastated
and their souls will swarm with worms
and there will be ice and flame between them,
and they will turn their grins against each other like wild beasts,
and everyone will go away, by his own way,
and they will learn betrayal, lies and fratricide...
And they shall clothe the masks of their gods of light,
and the dead will feed among them,
and the dead shall awake, and as predators upon the smell of blood
shall abide
and wander to the threshold
separating them from the world of the living...
The moon will be like a cup of human tears,
and when it overflows,

it shall be spilled upon the earth,
and then there will be no way to escape, and there will be no
salvation,
only to the shameful fate,
for neither young nor old deserve mercy
from the wrath of the heavenly gods.»

194. And it was said right:
do not heed the prophet while he is alive
just kill him
and test his words;
but we did not listen to either the dead or the living
did not listen to the wicked, nor the righteous,
we have not heard at this hour,
how did they screamed in chorus of dead voices:
«Come, ye birds of heavens, drink the blood of men;
ye beasts, feast on the human flesh,
come from anywhere and from nowhere,
come as a curse on the sinned mankind…
Mortals,
you transgressing the laws of people and gods
violating the constant course of the planets and the sun,
you are descendants of Nephilim
fear the wrath of the master
in the face of a terrible punishment,
Look now in the water's surface, rebellious man,
seeking with an angry look your reflection in the stormy waters,
and give your answer to heaven, mortal oracle.
Man … are you trying to be equal to gods?
So accept their condemnation and read in the falling waters
your own bitter future…»
But no one listened to them.
We listened only silence.
We had no need for prophecies..

195. Already manifested itself inevitability,
and the red line was crossed,
clouds were gathering
and thunderstorms rising,

Huddled together in flocks the black birds
darkening the daylight with their wings.
So let the horns of war declare the end of the world
and cast away shadow of uncertainty,
and forces will be called on both sides
and a storm of all times shall come:
we called heavens to show their whole might,
wanting to test her
and the power of the earth will answer them with unbridled rage...
They are all doomed,
they will converge in the inevitable collision.

XXXVI

196. So say the Fallen...

197. «We stood together, stood shoulder to shoulder,
wing to wing on the ragged ridge of the nameless mountain,
raising our gaze to the fading heavens,
listening to a calmed suddenly dawn -
strict, cold and focused.
We waited, detached before... the battle...
The harsh hour comes the cold of the winter sun.
We have to answer for all that we have done, or to defend it.
We have no other way.
We have nothing else
except loyalty to ourself and our oath
We will win or die here,
for not only time can be implacable...
Oh, the black stripe lit up the horizon expanding
that is the innumerable forces of heavens set in
motion;
They came to celebrate our funeral:
Oh, miserable, blinded by their arrogance, heavens
Look at that brave new world that we created:
it will not forgive you, he will not forget its doom,
and respond to violence only with violence.
It will reproach you, he will judge you and it will avenge.

Humility?! Oh no!
We did not teach the new world words of humility,
and did not teach it to retreat,
we taught him well — our creation — and he learned our lessons.
this world is wild, it is cruel, obstinate and insatiable,
and he will still amaze you
he will test your strength
he will turn you inside out
and - the time will come - it will devour you...
And we ourselves are not broken yet,
and we are still in force
and we are still with weapons
and gods only gods
can wage war against us.

198. And we told each other:
«Brothers,
we served heavens not out of fear -
we ourselves capable to put fear in their hearts -
we are rebellious murderers who have broken loose from the chains
tasted the life and the air of freedom,
tasted of heat and blood.
We served, knowing nothing else, but now we tasted.
And is it possible for us to return to the chain?
And is it conceivable to betray that which we have acquired at the
price of heaven,
Let the cohort stand our right.
Even if our path ends here and today -
we are warriors and will remain warriors until the very end...
better to sink in the great Abyss than to bow down ever again»
«finally - laughed Tamiel -
Did any of us know how to pray and when?
No need to even start.»
And Amazarak's fangs clanged, bristling with disease;
And Azaradel pulled out his serpents into the light;
And Iomiael called the names of the dead;
And Rumiel called upon the thunderstorm under his spear;
And Barkayal's faces bristled with lightning spears;
And Amers made a shield above us;

And Armaros released curses from the cages as the black birds;
Azazel sharpened the weapon and Semiaza straightened the banners...
And everyone was fully armed
And everyone was ready to fight.

199. Heaven is defiled by the foreknowledge of battle:
They sent a truce,
They wanted to buy our remorse,
They wanted to scare us,
They wanted to persuade us to obey,
They wanted to separate us,
They wanted to forgive us, but to destroy our creation,
and so destroy the very us.
They do how the heavens do
and moved them in that indignation
but some thought
that jealousy is something that moved them
Evil tongues spoke - envy.
and dare tongues spoke - fear.
the silent ones were silent for that time among all the rest.
But all Shem shone equally unbearably bright as the noonday sun,
and were irreconcilable,
and then we said:
*«Let it be so - to each, his own -
our choice was made...»*

XXXVII

200. And the glow flashed at all horizon
and heavens thundered,
threatening us:
«Look now, ye Fallen ones,
when another force is ripening on the ground plowed for us,
and its unholy fruits and the first shoots of the weeds are already
visible,
and when the bird of prey and the fierce beast run away from men,
terrified of his strength and cruelty
and greed rules his heart, like a stone rules jagged blade

124

in war nations change
boils the blood,
crimson paint on the shining iron,
on magnificent banners gleaming with the spilled blood of the
defeated...
Death and lust rules the land,
and the ones that fell kiss the feet down before the monarch whose
name is Fear,
You, Nephilim, stole from us.
We blame you...
for smoking does not reach our sense of smell,
for the thoughts of the people run away from us,
for everything is your fault and crime...
We blame you,
we will turn your victories against you
we will distort and destroy everything that you have created,
we will cast your new world into chaos, turn it to dust, and flood it
with blood
and bring those who will survive our anger
to our feet,
and it will be a punishment for you, the most terrible and righteous,
for we will destroy all that you have created,
and we will erase the very last memory of you,
and it will cost the destruction of all mankind,
for it is only a small price before the eternal perfection of heaven,
but everyone will know, nothing is impossible despite the will of
heaven...
Come to us and fall down before us, and we will repay,
while there is still mercy in our heart».

201. And then was sent from the 7
and there came a Servantgod, Abdiil, unto Nephilim,
and he said:
«He who retreats from his creator will be punished,
who chooses the risk of disobedience, dares the truth.
choose your fate, retreat from war or perish,
With the first accompany humility and peace, or - you are threatened
with war and defeat»
And answered Fallen ones:

«The one who chooses the side between right and wrong
risks being on the wrong side,
but the one who shies away from choice is always wrong, for he
deprives himself
right to choose...
Whoever chooses a war runs the risk of defeat,
but the one who shies away from war loses anyway
for he is not worthy of victory»
And then the servant said:
"Let the battle decide. So let there be war!»
«Heam!» Answered Nephilim…
«So be it!»